For Mothers *Raising Sons*

Lavelle Publishing

For Mothers *Raising Sons*

Robert Jackson

Lavelle Publishing

6600 Sugarloaf Pkwy • Suite 400-375 • Duluth, GA 30097
Website: www.robertjacksonmotivates.com
Email: info@robertjacksonmotivates.com

First Printing August 2023

No More Excuses: For Mothers Raising Sons

Paperback ISBN: 978-0-9659254-9-5

E-BOOK ISBN: 979-8-9888407-0-1

Library of Congress Control Number: 2023914651

Editor - Tajuana TJ Butler-Jackson

Copyeditor - Joy Scott Ressler and Carl Long

Cover Design - Tajuana TJ Butler-Jackson

Layout - Mehrab Meraj and Tajuana TJ Butler-Jackson

Cover Photo taken 1993 at Western Kentucky University - Bowling Green, Kentucky

Photo on back cover by Willie Peoples

Photo of Kym Whitley and Joshua - Source: Instagram

No More Excuses: For Mothers Raising Sons is available at special discounts when purchased in bulk for premiums and sales promotions as well as for fundraising or educational purposes. For details contact info@robertjacksonmotivates.com.

Table of Contents

In 2011, I became a mother to a son. A young lady I had been mentoring gave birth and left her baby with the hospital maternity ward—along with my name and phone number. Suddenly, I had one hour to decide. Would I adopt this girl's newborn? I said yes, named my new son, Joshua, and went about trying to figure out how to get over the fear of being a mom raising a son. As an actress and comedian, I have played numerous roles and it has come natural for me, but I didn't know the first thing about motherhood. I was fortunate to have friends, who I call my "village," to help me out. My son and I have grown tremendously since he came into my life over 12 years ago. Nonetheless, I still find myself questioning, "Am I doing this right?" After reading Robert's *For Mothers Raising Sons*, I wished I'd had this book from the start, but am fortunate to have it now as a reliable reference moving forward.

I'm my child's first teacher. So, I need strategies to better connect with him. This book gives solutions on how mothers can maintain a growth mindset versus a fixed mindset. Robert's book is a guide for any mother, aunt, cousin, sister or grandmother who is helping to raise sons, nephews, brothers or grandsons and need additional coaching on how to work through issues that will inevitably occur. Whether you are married or single, a working mom or stay at home mom, a seasoned mom or new mom, this book will drop some nuggets that will be helpful to you along your journey. Reading through the chapters, I was reassured of what I was doing right. Then Robert's no-nonsense approach of telling it like it is informed me of how to adjust my approach in the areas that I wasn't sure I was handling right.

How can our sons succeed without a foundation of respect, honesty, accountability, empathy, and safety? I have dated many men who have prompted the question in my head, "Who raised him?" Women always want great qualities in the men they date but aren't raising their sons to be great men someone else's daughter will date. We must set high expectations for our sons. We must expect them to meet and exceed the standard set before them. It is our job to create an environment in which our sons feel safe enough to come to us. They need to know that we will do our best to guide them and equip them with the knowledge and tools that they need. We must help them to not only tackle the obstacles before them, but also to flourish and become the individuals they are called to be. Many young men are influenced by outside forces. Toxic masculinity has become the norm. As moms, we can combat this mentality and first teach our sons that it's okay to show emotion. We must also teach them to control their emotions.

Don't get me wrong, I have made my share of mistakes. For example, when Joshua was younger, he would ask for juice at midnight. Initially I was like, "Oh, I would never give him juice at night." I ended up giving him a little juice and little water. Or he was like, "Can I watch TV?" I was like, "No." He goes, "Just a little bit?" "Oh, OK." Those were minor but no means no, not maybe. Another example is not teaching him to use the restroom standing until my brother noticed he was sitting at 5 years old! At the end of the day, I have learned that we can't do anything about what we have already done, therefore it isn't healthy to beat ourselves up because of any mistakes we've made. Mr. Jackson says in his book, "There are no perfect parents." Instead of focusing on being a perfect parent, it is important that we simply be who our sons need us to be. Their needs will vary from year to year as they age, and from day to day as they experience life's challenges. Our goal should be to be there for them and to help guide them through the tough times.

Also, we can't control every situation. Emotional Intelligence means managing my emotions while managing (not controlling) the emotions of my son and the others around me. Many of us lose control and our kids catch the brunt. This book addresses how to cope in those situations and provides solutions for how to prevent them from happening. In the book, Robert shares that if our emotions are not intact, our sons' emotions won't be either. For me, I have had to learn to control my own emotions in order to become the example that my son needs me to be. I encourage other mothers to do the same.

We can't be good to our sons if we're not good to ourselves. Self-care is a must. That starts with showing love for self, which Robert discusses in detail in the book. However, we can't neglect accountability, which is equally important. The Mama's

Boy chapter will have mothers challenging themselves to do better because a lot of us are guilty of coddling and protecting instead of trusting and encouraging.

For Mothers Raising Sons covers so many areas that we face while raising our sons. Sometimes we make choices concerning our boys without giving them enough consideration. This book motivates you to consider your actions and it helps you to help your son embrace his individuality. It provides strategies on how to connect with our sons in a world of social media and cell phones. Robert has laid out pertinent examples of how to handle and address blatant disrespect from our sons. He makes it clear that if your son doesn't feel a connection of good communication and synergy with you, he will seek it elsewhere; and elsewhere may be an undesirable source.

I endorse *For Mothers Raising Sons* and I appreciate the message. One of my favorite chapters is How Boys and Men Think. As women, I think we could all use a crash course in this subject alone. Enjoy this book and practice the strategies that Robert Jackson has laid out. We all want to effectively raise our sons to become successful men. This book is the right tool at the right time to help us out.

Kym Whitley is an American film and television actress and comedienne.

I wrote *For Mothers Raising Sons* for mothers who are seeking the proper way to raise their sons. Many moms have ongoing questions about rearing their sons and are looking for answers. In many cases, mothers subconsciously and unintentionally do things that negatively affect their sons. My goal is to challenge you to take an honest look at yourself while confronting your thought processes. Doing so will motivate you to properly assist your son with his growth.

This book is for all mothers with sons whether they are married, single, living at home or on their own. It doesn't matter if he is in college or part of the workforce. Whether he is young or middle-aged, or if he is heterosexual or homosexual, this book will give you tools that work. Whatever your race, ethnicity, or background, this book is for you. The issues young men go through vary; however, many of their experiences are similar.

You may feel that you have a great relationship with your son, nephews, male cousins, etc. If that is the case, that's wonderful. I commend you, but no one knows everything. While reading you may find some nuggets that will assist you or answer questions you might have. You may be propelled to take actions you didn't realize needed to be taken or that have long been overdue. If you are a mother, a grandmother, an aunt, or a caretaker of a man, young or old, this book is for you. If you are searching for ways to reach your son, this book is for you. If you are trying to figure out when to let go and let him grow, this book was written for you!

Introduction

Young men go through different emotions, so it's important that you empathize with your son and how he feels. Understanding him is necessary because many men, young and old, hide their emotions. There's a good chance your son experiences an identity crisis daily, especially if his father isn't present in his life. He questions who he is, who he is supposed to be and who he will become. Wouldn't you feel more empowered if you possessed the tools to properly raise your young son? Wouldn't it be helpful to know how to address problems with your older son to help him successfully navigate the pitfalls and struggles he will surely encounter as he matures? Instilling the right tools early will provide a better future for him, his future family, and maybe even you, his mother.

Despite various stressful situations in life, it is necessary for you to take an honest look in the mirror to determine what steps need to be taken, both in your life and in your son's life. This effort will ensure that your son has a chance to become an adult who not only knows how to survive but is capable of prospering. You have the ability to guide and help prepare him to face any challenge he may encounter. To do so, you must first understand that there is a way to communicate and gain your son's respect. It starts by knowing who your son is as a person and how he thinks.

To relate to you, your son first needs a better understanding of who his mother is as a person. Some sons never comprehend their mother's true makeup. A lot of mothers are in so much emotional pain and turmoil from being abused by their parents or the men in their lives that they directly or indirectly transfer that pain to their sons. The pain manifests itself when mothers degrade their sons in public for making simple mistakes. Then he is further alienated when his mother stresses him out—yelling, cursing, and telling him he isn't worth anything. This happens when mothers are emotionally unavailable when their sons need a listening ear. It is demonstrated when mothers don't discipline consistently. Instead, they explode out of anger once they've allowed their sons' actions to build up animosity over time. At worst, some mothers let a man abuse them right in their sons' presence.

Other mothers may appear to be selfish and prideful whether they intend to or not. These mothers spend a considerable amount of time getting their hair, nails and eyelashes done. Some buy clothes they can't afford, go out to clubs, and/or use drugs or controlled substances. Others don't have the time or resources to invest in their sons' extracurricular activities, sporting events, or personal development. Because of multiple and unnecessary reasons, such as feeling disrespected, misunderstood, or attempting to send a message about who is in charge, some mothers deprive their sons of basic needs like food and shelter. Nobody is perfect, so if any of these examples apply to you, don't be too hard on yourself. Instead, be open and willing to learn a better way to relate to and care for your son.

If your husband is in the house, he should share the responsibility of raising your son, but sometimes fathers are emotionally unavailable. Whether he is there or not, you still have the responsibility of doing your part. Unfortunately, if mothers do not wisely choose how they rear their sons, the fates of their sons are sealed. The numbers don't lie. The following are a few sobering statistics to help you see what you must rally against.

If you are raising an African American or Latino male, you must combat him falling into unsavory situations that don't end well. According to the U.S. Department of Justice, young men of color are:

- 30% more likely to be pulled over by police
- 3 times more likely to be searched
- Shot by police at twice the rate of whites
- Arrested at twice the rate of whites
- 75% more likely to be charged than white males
- Sentenced to longer prison terms than whites

- 44% of the nation's homicides
- 30% of US population but 46% of the nations prison population

Also, be aware that:

- 1 out of 22 die from homicide
- 1 out of 6 are arrested before age 19
- Over half released from prison return within 3 years (Possession of Drugs, Theft, Robbery, Burglary)
- 77% of all felony cases are solved with a plea deal

Men of Color have:

- The highest retention rate amongst all students
- The highest in school and out of school suspensions and expulsions
- A lack of support in social factors, education, employment, health, and criminal justice

There is an all-out assault on young men of color in this country. Prepared mothers have a better opportunity to save their sons. If your son doesn't fall into any of the categories mentioned, he will still face tough challenges and circumstances. This is not a time to panic. This is a time to inform yourselves, so that you can guide your sons, young and old, with confidence and significant influence instead of control and force.

Here is one of my favorite quotes from Dr. Carter G Woodson's book, *The Mis-Education of the Negro*:

"If you can control a man's thinking, you do not have to concern yourself with his actions. When you determine what a man shall think, you do not have to concern yourself about what he will do. If you make a man feel inferior, you do not have to compel him to accept an inferior status, he will seek it himself. If you make a man think he is justly an outcast, you won't have to order him to the back door. He will go without being told; and if there is no back door, his very nature will demand one."

With that being said, your goal should be to ensure your son knows how to properly assess situations and make informed decisions for himself. When you try to control your son's thinking, you are damaging and destroying his ability to learn to think for himself. You will not always be there to think for him. He must learn to do so on his own. It is your job to teach him from an early age to be confident enough to respectfully speak and eventually think for himself. Additionally, if he is exposed to negativity daily, negativity will control his thinking and actions. Your assignment as his mother is to help him find his greatness, including his identity and his purpose! Controlling him will only cause him more pain and suffering down the line. The thought process of our young men is already influenced by other outside factors like social media, television, music, peer pressure, school influences, etc. As he matures, he shouldn't run to you to make decisions for him, instead he needs you to be a haven and a significant role model from whom to receive sound counsel.

I have witnessed too many young men lacking self-sufficiency, self-motivation, a sense of history and a sense of hope. Several are misguided, angry, frustrated, and conditioned to accept less, with no motivation to get it right. Being unkempt, skipping school and not reading or studying has become the norm. All the while, young men are falling further behind in comprehending and retaining the fundamentals of basic manhood.

Some young men have trouble with friendships and relationships, so they follow the wrong crowd to get what they misperceive as respect. Your son may feel pressured to have sex because all his friends are doing it. His peers may drink alcohol and beer or smoke marijuana. Maybe he's doing his best to resist the temptation, but the pressure is mounting. Your son may try to get his head together but doesn't know how. He might try to make the best decisions for his life and attempt to stay on track, but he goes to school and doesn't feel understood, heard, or seen by his teachers or peers. Some sons feel sorry for themselves but blame others instead of taking responsibility for their actions. Others have given up on themselves, quitting anything in their lives that could bring them value or meaning.

You should take deliberate actions to properly educate your son and prepare him to overcome and succeed beyond the difficulties he may one day find himself faced with. This responsibility is crucial, whether you carried him for nine months, adopted him, or you just took on the role of caretaker. Every young man is one caring adult away from being a success story. He must be taught discipline and accountability, preferably at a young age. Your thoughtful intervention and guidance could potentially prevent, or at the very least decrease the number of males being gunned down in the streets and filling prison cells.

There may be a mother reading this book who has lost her son. I empathize with you because the laws and life are not always fair. Everyone doesn't look at your son as valuable. Some police officers and educators don't value the lives of young men of color. Even still, based on their actions, some mothers don't seem to value the lives of their sons either. Others don't realize their role in the raising of a misguided young man, or the repercussions of raising him irresponsibly. There are some innocent young men that fall victim to homicide or suicide, and it hurts, but sometimes our young men put themselves in bad situations.

I saw a story on the news where a nineteen-year-old young man had broken into an elderly woman's home while she was asleep. As he climbed through her window, she shot him with her gun. He died on the scene. He never completed his mission of entering her home; although there are numerous scenarios that could have played out as a result of him trespassing. He could have sexually assaulted her, killed her, or robbed her. He definitely wasn't breaking in to take out her trash. Consequently, she didn't wait around to see what his intentions were. Instead, she took action, which she was well within her rights to do. As the saying goes, she shot first and asked questions later. When the news covered the story, the young man's mom and sister were outraged. They said that she didn't have to shoot him. They thought she should have called the police.

Where is the accountability? Who was responsible for this young man's ignorance and careless behavior? Based on their comments, both his mother and sister condoned his behavior.

Neither of the women held him accountable for his reckless actions. Neither his mom nor sister acknowledged that he shouldn't have broken into the woman's home. They only made excuses for him.

A mother not holding her son accountable for his actions will destroy his character and hinder his growth. We don't know why he chose to burglarize this woman's home, but we can assume, based on her reaction, that it wasn't a decision that was strongly opposed by his mother. Why didn't she see the error of his ways? You don't get a gold star or pat on the back for stealing someone else's property. There are consequences for bad choices. This mother was wrong to make excuses for her son. She enabled him. She even mentioned to the news reporter that he needed money and that's why he did what he did. Her judgement was faulty. That statement alone revealed the mother's inability to properly guide her son. Apparently she doesn't understand that both she and her son looked at life through a distorted lens. Mothers tend to defend their sons even when they know they are wrong, which is an example of bad parenting. This young man paid the ultimate price. I can only imagine what kind of misguidance he received growing up that led him to his death at such a young age.

The school-to-prison pipeline is real. More and more young men of color are being prepped for prison instead of college. This path often starts at home, not school. Calling the police on your son because you can't control your emotions, or his, will only lead him to prison faster. Your actions often decide his fate. You decide his fate every time you allow him to get away with ignorant behavior without consistent discipline. You decide his fate every time you turn a blind eye when he is disrespectful to others. You decide his fate when you are too preoccupied with your own social life or personal needs. You decide his fate when he comes to you to express his feelings and emotions and you shut him out by not listening. You decide his fate when his teacher calls you to discuss a plan for his education and you never return calls or show up for parent-teacher conferences or answer their emails. Instead, you complain about his teachers and his education, claiming they are not doing enough. I agree that some schools are failing to meet the needs of our young men. However, parents need to hold themselves accountable to have their sons prepared. It's very simple: take the important and necessary steps to learn how to properly raise and guide your son to be the man that you desire him to be.

Treating Young Sons Like Grown Men

Chapter 1

Mothers often treat their sons like husbands or boyfriends. Women who do this typically have a void in their life or the man is not in the house. If he is in the house, he is emotionally or financially unavailable for her and her children, which has long term effects on both mother and son. Uncomfortable with their forced role as head of the household, some mothers feel like they desperately need help handling the responsibility so they lean heavily on their sons. Others simply feel like it's not a woman's responsibility to do a man's job. So, they put adult male responsibilities, that are generally held by men her age or older, on their sons at a very young age. This forced maturity leads to early anxiety, PTSD, nervousness, anger and disrespectful behavior among other consequences. Such high expectations can be devastating to a young man as he deals with his mother's disregard for his childhood to look out for her own needs and apparent shortcomings.

Some examples of adult male responsibilities that are put on young men include paying utilities, rent and their mother's car payment monthly or several times a year. Some young men are also expected to take care of younger siblings for extended periods of time, give baths, cook dinner, clean the entire home, provide discipline and wash clothes for the household. Some sons must also provide emotional support by listening to their mothers complain and gripe about their father, her friends, ex-boyfriends and what is lacking in the household or her life. Countless young men are plagued with many of these burdens on a consistent basis. Such emotional weight causes unnecessary stress.

Instead of paying bills with the money they earn, young men should be able to buy their own school clothes, a bike, school supplies, tennis shoes and other necessary items. A savvy mother would take the extra step and find a program for him to learn how to invest and save his money. Expecting, forcing, or guilting your sons into paying your family's light bill, gas bill, water bill, rent or mortgage, food, cable, and phone bill places him in the role as the head of the household, which clearly isn't his responsibility.

Too often, mothers put bills in their sons' names before they are old enough to speak for themselves or build their credit. If the mother is irresponsible and fails to keep the bill current, her son's credit is destroyed before he can even begin to understand its purpose or how to utilize it. Giving too much responsibility to your sons is not the answer. It should be you, and/or your husband or significant other who assumes the responsibility as the head of your household.

Reasonably, your son should have duties at your home, including taking out the trash, cleaning his room, and cleaning the kitchen or living room. However, maintaining the cleanliness of an entire household is overwhelming for a young man or any child. Watching his siblings from time to time is good practice. However, when his siblings look to him as their caretaker, that is an excessive amount of responsibility. This causes anxiety in young men that carries into their adult years.

It is healthy to develop a conversational relationship with your son to share the events of your day and to have him share the events of his. It becomes unhealthy when the conversation ends up turning into a venting fest with a mother complaining about her friend cheating on her boyfriend with his best friend, her ex-boyfriend trying to get back with her even though he "ain't worth shit," or his dad being trifling and not paying child support. This information is better left to be shared with another adult, or better yet, a counselor who can help you make more sound decisions.

Some mothers have a history of watching their own mother or grandmother repeat the same cycle of behavior, or maybe a mother watched her cousins or aunts treat their sons this way. Maybe her brother was treated as the man of the house, even though he was a kid, so she feels justified. Maybe she didn't have a lot of strong men in her family, so early on she put her son in the position to be the man she wanted in her life. These scenarios are common in many broken families.

As mothers rely on their sons, their relationship begins to resemble that of boyfriend and girlfriend or husband and wife. Outside of sharing a bed, they share everything that is a part of a romantic relationship. This can be confusing for both the son and the mother. The bond that is formed seems normal until the son reaches the age where he is ready to become involved in a true romantic relationship and receives resentment and resistance from his mother.

According to Kenneth Adams, the author of *SilentlySeduced: When Parents Make Their Children Partners,* "Covert incest occurs when a child becomes the object of a parent's affection, love, passion, and preoccupation." Covert incest, also known as emotional incest, is a type of abuse that occurs when a parent looks to their child for the emotional support that would be normally provided by another adult. Adams further shares that, "The parent, motivated by the loneliness and emptiness created by a chronically troubled marriage or relationship, makes the child a surrogate partner. The boundary between caring love and incestuous love is crossed when the relationship with the child exists to meet the needs of the parent rather than those of the child." Some mothers unknowingly treat their sons as their significant other rather than maintaining a parental relationship with their sons, and this confusion damages young men and eventually causes resentment toward their moms.

A mother is dependent on her son when her responses to him become increasingly desperate and jealous. It shows disregard for his personal boundaries. She manipulates her son to avoid the heartache that is a result of her own troubled or failed marriage or relationship. In exchange, a son becomes preoccupied with his mother's needs and becomes overprotective and overly concerned. Adams says, "A psychological marriage between parent and child results; the child becomes the parent's surrogate spouse." When emotional incest occurs, a mother's emotional needs are being met but her sons' needs aren't, so he grows up with an inability to control his emotions. In some cases, he is not in touch with his emotions at all. Further, this unfair treatment through the years from a mother to her unsuspecting son causes him to eventually resent women in his future relationships, including her.

Mothers Marinating in Pain

I'm sure most mothers have no idea the damage that takes place when they treat their sons with mental and physical cruelty due to their own pain. You may not love yourself like you should. Maybe you don't know any other way. You may be callous and intentionally hurt your son. As the saying goes, hurt people hurt people. Whatever the case, you may want it to stop but don't know how. As adults, we are all products of our own decisions, whether good or bad. It is your choice to continue to be controlled by your pain or decide to overcome it to have healthier dealings with your son.

Mothers, the first thing you must understand is the pain will leave you whenever you are ready for it to leave. It's a choice. Pain is temporary. Mental pain is an emotion. When you decide to break up with the pain, you must be willing to put in the work necessary to understand and face the cause, forgive, begin the healing process, and move on. Divorce yourself from past pain and stop allowing it to influence your behavior.

When you adopt the mindset that says, "This pain I'm experiencing has to go," your actions will line up with it. We all have been hurt in past relationships. If you are marinating in your own pain, get to the origin or the root of that pain. What caused you this turmoil? What have you done to come to grips with your stress and pain? You can't do anything about what has already been done. What was the lesson in it? Never come out of a troubled situation without wisdom. Find someone to speak with about the pain. Seek counseling. If you are still in the midst of the conflict, make it a priority to find resources to help you cope and begin the work of healing.

QUESTIONS TO ASK TO GET TO THE ROOT OF YOUR PAIN

1. What caused my turmoil?
2. What have I done to come to grips with my stress and pain?
3. What lesson did I learn?

When a person is hurt about something, they often put that hurt on the people closest to them, whether they intend to or not. When mothers have children while they are in emotional pain, stress and duress, their children absorb it. It leads to future problems for your son, with his teachers, and others who encounter him. These problems are caused by the pain you are conditioning him to accept. Mothers, don't you want to feel whole for once in your life? Do you want to continue to inflict pain on your children?

If you are ready to change, a good place to begin the healing process is to face the things you are stressed out about.

Top Stresses for Parents

1. Money
2. Maintaining a household
3. School preparation
4. Homework
5. Bedtime routine
6. Healthy meal choices

Managing stress is key to getting the mental break that you need. When you are stressed, you stress out your children. Their stress leads to behavioral issues at school, unfriendly interactions with others, or self-hate. To break the cycle, it is important to manage your own stress while teaching your children how to deal with theirs.

Before you can overcome stress, you must first understand what stress is. The Britannica Dictionary defines stress as a state of mental tension and worry caused by problems in your life, work, etc. Stress is something that causes strong feelings of worry, anxiety, physical force, or pressure. Stress is a state of mind that can cause diseases or even kill you!

Stress occurs when you are on the job and in your everyday life. When you have mental and emotional strain on your brain, it will cause you to agitate yourself and other people. Treating your son like your boyfriend or husband will not help you deal with this stress or your pain. It will pass your pain onto your son.

4 Steps to Overcoming Pain

1. **You must acknowledge it.** Point to yourself and say, "I'm in pain!" Recognize that you have been wronged, treated inappropriately, misused, or overlooked by people or a particular person in your life. Acknowledge that an unfortunate circumstance left you mentally and spiritually wounded. Face the pain and accept that your pain has caused you to react unfavorably toward people who you encounter.
2. **You must write it down.** Writing down on paper what the pain stems from, who caused it, and the circumstances around it helps you to pinpoint the core of the pain. It helps you to release it through a more thoughtful approach. Also, write down affirmations encouraging yourself to overcome your previous circumstance(s). Write positive statements such as, *I am an overcomer of negative encounters, I am a conqueror. I am worthy to overcome this incident. I am victorious.*
3. **You must speak to someone you trust.** You cannot trust everyone, so it's important that you share this information with someone who will be sensitive to your feelings and needs and will keep your information confidential. This person could be a mentor, pastor, counselor, co-worker, or family member who will

protect your feelings and give you sound instruction or advice.

4. **You must seek to forgive.** When you are in pain, odds are the pain is the residue of an incident in which someone wronged you. Forgiving that person is more for your well-being than anything else. To forgive, you must step outside of your own pain and attempt to comprehend what must have been going on in that person's life to have caused him or her to lash out at you. When you forgive someone for hurting you, it releases the negative energy you have held onto for so many years. You never forget what happened, but at least you can forgive so you can move forward with your life.

Kids will observe how you handle stress and respond accordingly. There are a multitude of people running around in pain, wanting to do something about it, but not knowing how. It's time to break this cycle of distress and anguish. If you don't address it, you will continue to marinate in that pain. Emotional pain can be felt in your head, your heart, and your stomach. It comes out through your words and your actions toward other people. Your son deserves a mother who is making every attempt to be healthy and whole. He needs his mother to help him work through his own pain, some of which she may have caused directly or indirectly. If you don't deal with your pain, you will continue to inflict it on him. However, if you find the courage to face and work through your own pain, you will heal for yourself and you will also become a much-needed healthy influence in your son's life.

Allow Your Son to Have a Childhood

Why are so many mothers so comfortable treating their young sons like grown men? Then, when he acts like a grown man at the wrong time, his mother punishes him, even inciting a verbal or physical altercation. Make up your mind; you can't have it both ways. I can speak about this from personal experience. Ever since I was a kid, I was treated like a man because there wasn't a consistent man in my home. My mother had four girls and I was her only son, and although I wasn't the oldest child, I reluctantly found myself in the role of co-head of household. I felt like a man at times, and sometimes I felt like a kid, which was confusing for me. Because of the missing male figure, my mother leaned on me. I felt like I had to assert myself as a man and she didn't stop me, but when I had to take on the role of a child, it was difficult for me to turn it off.

When your son is watching his mother or siblings struggling and suffering, his instincts kick in. Instincts take over no matter your son's age. His brain sends a response saying, "I have to do something," or "I need to help my family with these bills," or "I have to help put some food on the table." He is not thinking about the stress he is enduring, in the midst of it all. His body and brain move into fight-or-flight, and he doesn't hesitate to act, especially when there is no one else present to do so. Most young men don't think before acting, they just act!

I was 8 or 9 years old putting food on the table. I made money by cutting grass, raking leaves, shoveling snow, carrying groceries, delivering newspapers and pumping gas. I worked all day on Saturdays and sometimes after school during the week. Even though my mother didn't pressure me to help out,

I saw a need and went about filling it. I bought groceries and paid bills. In high school, most other kids did homework or played video games. After practice I worked at various fast-food restaurants out of necessity.

When a responsible young man sees his mother crying, her struggle at that moment becomes his priority. Watching TV, playing video games, or hanging with friends all take a back seat. He becomes concerned that, if he doesn't do something right away, his family will be living in the streets or in a shelter. His main objective becomes figuring out his options to help see his mother smile again by helping his family come out of a bad situation. As he watches the pressure mount on his mother, all he wants to do is step up and do something about it.

If you share with your son the pressures that you deal with as a single mom providing for your family, that stress is being put on your son unfairly, even if you are doing this unintentionally. I don't believe mothers intend to put that stress on their sons, treating them like grown men with responsibilities. Her allowing him to help often happens unconsciously because a real man, even though he's a young man, is not going to watch his mom struggle without attempting to help. He'll figure out a way to provide an income even if he feels that he must turn to illegal outlets like selling drugs, robbing people, etc. It's a lot of pressure to provide when you are not being provided for.

When I was growing up, I didn't fully understand manhood, but I knew manhood wasn't what I was seeing from the men in my mother's life. I thought that manhood was about stepping up to the plate when you were needed the most. To me it was about paying the bills and putting your family's minds at ease and their needs above your own. It was about providing so there would be food on the table consistently without lame excuses. The men in my life up to that point seemed weak and were always making excuses for their immature behavior. They were not good providers and lacked motivation, and they were not exhibiting the best examples of manhood.

When I had to step up and provide for my mother and our household, I did not realize the effects that missing my childhood would have on me later in life. The stress on me was so overwhelming that I didn't know how to turn it off at school. I felt like most of my teachers were insensitive to my home situation or at least acted as if they didn't care. When a teacher would yell at me, I would say something back and get kicked out of class. I was playing the man of the house role at home already. While my teacher was asking me about a pencil, I was thinking, *Does she even know what we are dealing with at home? How dare she say something about me forgetting my pencil? We almost didn't eat last night. Why is she nitpicking about a pencil?*

My mother mixing up my roles in the house left me confused and angry. I was used to being a leader in my house. However, my mom and I would have disagreements because I would forget which role I needed to operate in at any given time. I was treated like the man of the house one minute and her son the next. I wasn't mature enough to turn my emotions off at home or at school. It was a constant power struggle that I wasn't equipped to handle.

Allow your son to have a childhood. Allow him to mature at his own pace and allow him to remain a child until he is old enough and ready for manhood. Frequently, young mothers find themselves growing up with their sons. They are trying to figure out life while trying to raise a child and are unsure how to juggle the two. I understand and suggest that you keep the two separate. When your son tries to help when your bills are due or food is scarce, reassure him that you have it covered even if you don't. Remember **the five P**'s: **P**roper **P**reparation **P**revents **P**oor **P**erformance. Seek help from local government agencies, churches, and other community outreach programs if you are in need of food, shelter or a job.

In attempting to build a life for yourself and your family, be proactive instead of reactive. If your son's father isn't present, take the steps necessary to ensure that he pays child support. He should also help provide emotional support to your son by spending time with him. Schedule that time and encourage him to follow through. Don't allow your personal feelings toward him to dictate his relationship with his son. Breakups can be ugly but be the bigger person. Think about your son's needs. If the father is in the home, challenge him to become more emotionally available to his son. If he's not employed, encourage him to seek gainful employment. If he doesn't have any skills, suggest that he seek a trade program or apprenticeship training that will lead to a stable career. If he can't provide emotional and financial support to you and your son, why is he there?

The Effects of Treating Your Sons Like Grown Men

When you treat your son like he's your husband or boyfriend, it affects him significantly, both short and long term. Short term, it causes him preventable stress and affects his dealings with others. He doesn't fully understand that he's being treated like a man yet, but he feels all the anxiety and emotions that come with it. Long term, as he gets older it affects his relationships, not only with you, but also with the women who will eventually enter his life.

When you lean on him too much for emotional support, he grows up and realizes that he may not want to be in an adult relationship because he just wants a period of time where he is not responsible for anyone other than himself. There is a good chance that he will become resentful because he feels he missed his childhood.

Personally, when I became an adult, I avoided serious relationships because I didn't want any emotional or financial obligation for once in my life. At a time when I should have been preparing to pursue a significant other, I was emotionally drained and I didn't have the mental capacity to handle a serious relationship. I felt burned out as a young man. During the first few years that I was an undergrad at Western Kentucky University, I chose to hold off pursuing any serious romantic relationships. I put my emphasis on making good grades, playing football and running track. Eventually, at the end of my sophomore year, I tried having a girlfriend, but I wished I had stuck to my original plan because I was reminded of having to be responsible for someone else's well-being and I wasn't ready for that. I wasn't emotionally prepared. It was draining. Relationships take work and I was still rebounding from the weight of my childhood responsibilities.

I lost a few good relationships because I was emotionally detached. One of the young ladies I dated wanted a commitment. She was ready to be in a serious relationship, but it felt to me more like a marriage than a friendly, loving relationship. I constantly felt like I didn't have time just to get to know myself and my needs. I felt like she wanted to occupy any free time I had to myself outside of class or sports games and practices. I just wanted to breathe. I didn't know who I was or what I wanted to do and I knew that I wouldn't be any good to anyone if I didn't tend to myself. How can you be in a relationship with someone else when you don't even know who you are?

In my adult years, my mother was ill with kidney failure and continued to treat me more like her husband than her son. Although I love my mother and was empathetic to her health and knew she needed to lean on me, I always resented that treatment. I became apathetic with women I was with intimately. I felt like some men were further along in their thought process and had the capacity to better handle a serious relationship. I assumed they had more favorable home-life experiences. I felt at a disadvantage because I never knew what it was like to be free from being obligated to someone. I made my position clear. If someone seemed to get too clingy or attached, I would say, "I thought you said you just wanted to be friends." or "I thought you just wanted to hang out." I didn't sugar coat the situation. The truth was the truth. Some of the ladies I dated felt like I was being rude because I was too straight forward, speaking my mind freely about the status of our relationship. One of my past girlfriends told me, "You just want to be a player."

That wasn't my goal. I didn't want to hurt anyone's feelings; I just didn't know how to process the angst that I felt growing up. I wasn't ready to continue sharing the responsibility that I had to share with my mother when I wasn't ready or equipped to do so. I didn't want to relive the anxiety. I simply didn't want to be a reliable source let alone have to provide an answer to being questioned about where I had been. I wanted to hang out with the guys. I needed a break from the unspoken demands of the needs of the household in which I grew up in and going to college gave me that break. I wasn't about to let the demands of a young lady who I wasn't sure if I wanted to spend any considerable amount of time with disturb that. As I matured into manhood, I later learned to practice altruism in relationships.

When a young man has zero gas in his tank, the clueless young lady receives little to no emotional reciprocity. Your son might feel how I did. He may be staying away from serious relationships because he feels as though he had already been married for 18 years. From my encounters, when most women graduate from college or reach a certain age, they are understandably ready to get married. On the other side of that, if a young man has been treated like he's been married his whole life, it changes his ability to step up to the plate and meet young ladies at their level. Due to the duress he was under from having to step into an adult role at a young age, he lacks emotional, physical, or psychological cognition in this area. In some cases, by the time a man has recuperated and is ready to settle down and get married, the one he really wanted to marry eventually or should have married is long gone.

Although some mothers don't push their sons to support her and their family, she still tends to allow him to provide if he continues to take it upon himself to do so. Mothers, Grandmothers and Aunts, please understand that if you're treating your son like a man at a young age, it will cause psychological damage. Darius Cikanavicus shares in the article, "The Effects of Trauma from Growing up Too Fast," that growing up too fast or being mature beyond your years is often seen as a neutral or even a positive thing. In actuality, it is a psychological prison that the child is put into by their caregivers where they are expected to be perfect, meet unrealistic standards, or fit into a role that doesn't belong to them.

If you have treated your son like an adult and didn't realize it, pull him to the side and talk to him. Apologize to him for not understanding the ramifications of giving him responsibilities beyond his years. On the other hand, if he comes to you to talk about how he felt unfairly treated growing up, remember it's his story, not yours. Be sensitive to his story and perspective by practicing good listening without emotion and without interrupting or being defensive. Don't try to correct him or discredit his version of his story growing up. Like him, your perspective could be based on your feelings versus the facts. Apologize to him and let him know that causing him to grow up too fast wasn't your intention and that you did the best you could.

Ways to Heal and Move Forward from Treating Your Son Like an Adult

1. Don't feel sorry for yourself and take it personally. It is more important to forgive yourself with humility, not pride.

2. Admit your mistakes. Recognize what took place and try not to repeat the behavior with him or your other children.

3. Sit down and have a conversation with your son. Share with him that you realize that you have put too much pressure on him regarding family financial problems and/or your own personal issues.

4. Ask him how he feels. Allow him to speak freely, uninterrupted.

5. Validate what he has shared and will share in the future with you by letting him know you understand. Even if you don't agree, let him know that his feelings are valid and valued.

6. Move forward. Make a conscious effort to monitor the kinds of conversations that you have with your sons and around your sons. Continue to treat him like a son.

7. Be more positive when engaging with your son. Try to direct your conversations toward helping him plan his future or talk about positive things you'd like to do to improve yourself. Speak life into yourself and into him with daily positive affirmations.

What is a Mama's Boy?

A mama's boy is a man who is excessively influenced or attached to his mother. He doesn't make any decisions without checking in with his mom first. When making plans with his partner, he says things like, "This sounds like a good plan, but let me check with my mom to see what she thinks first." Some mothers never cut the emotional umbilical cord and regrettably raise a mama's boy fully dependent on his mother rather than himself. Some young men have attempted to cut the umbilical cord but their mother continues to hold on for dear life, feeling like she will miss out if she's not involved.

I'm not referring to young men under the age of 18 or men with special needs or other disabilities. For example, men who have autism or other mental illnesses need to be dependent on someone for their survival, whether it's their mother or another family member. When I use the term "mama's boy," I'm referring to healthy, adult males who never separate from their mother mentally and emotionally.

Don't get me wrong. Moms, you are very helpful in certain situations. You give great advice at times, but at some point, you must allow your grown son to be a man and make his own decisions without your approval. If he is married or in a serious relationship, it's healthy to encourage him to talk to his spouse, or significant other, to make the right choices for his family or his situation before coming you. He is not a child anymore. His wife, too, is a grown woman and a contributor to the decisions in their household. Her opinion counts. Don't make derogatory comments about her for no reason, even if she makes mistakes. Respect that he leans on her for advice. He is supposed to lean on her because they have become one.

A personal example of how a mama's boy relationship can stifle a son's ability to grow is an old friend of mine with whom I went to grade school and high school. His mom always coddled him when we were kids, but we didn't think much of it at the time. (Moms tend to do that with their sons, especially single moms.) As we got older, it never stopped. She made all his decisions for him. She cooked and washed his clothes, even when he was in his 30s. He did get married for a short period of time, but after the divorce he moved back in with her and they seemed to have picked up right where they left off. He is over 50 now and still lives in her basement. She isn't ill and neither is he; both are perfectly healthy physically but are mentally and emotionally attached. She is still cooking, cleaning and washing his clothes for him. He doesn't have a good relationship with his children. As far as I know, he hasn't made any strides to improve financially and does just enough to get by.

Showing affection to demonstrate your love toward someone and coddling them are two different things. Mothers, love your sons with all your heart, but don't coddle them. Coddling means to spoil or pamper someone. It starts when your kids are still babies, and it goes on into adulthood without stopping. Some mothers may say, *What seems to be the problem? How my son and I choose to govern our lives is our own business.*

You are correct, it is your business. However, consider just how such a relationship could hinder your son's ability to mature. When a mother controls her sons' life, it prevents him from ever seeing what he is capable of becoming, because he will never fully develop and grow into the man he could have been. Men were meant to be leaders of households and communities. How many men are not walking in their calling because they lack the tools and intellect to achieve the goals that are buried within him? Many goals, dreams and aspirations die in the minds of a grown boy living in the basement of his mother's house.

Why Women Complain

A lot of women complain about dating mama's boys. These men have been enabled so much that they don't step up as men when needed. If you are in good health, your mature son shouldn't be living with you. He is not your man. He is your son. Some mothers are lonely and enjoy the company. I get it, but it's still not right. It's okay to cook for him from time to time, but making breakfast, lunch and dinner daily and watching movies together sounds more like he is a romantic partner rather than your son. He could visit from time to time, and there is nothing wrong with sharing dinner or a movie with you, but this shouldn't be a daily occurrence.

A woman wants a man who takes care of himself first and can stand on his own two feet; a man who is confident enough to make his own decisions; a man who helps her feel accepted, significant, secure, and who affirms her and her purpose.

Signs You're Creating a Mama's Boy

There is a thin line dividing a son's close relationship with his mom, himself and his significant other. Whether the father is present or not, you must monitor your close relationship with your son and make sure it's not becoming unhealthy. Speaking to him 4 to 5 times a day over the phone, being upset when he dates other women, spoiling him, constantly giving him money even though he has his own job and resources, making excuses for his immature and ignorant behavior are all signs of having an unsound emotional attachment to your son.

It is not healthy if your son runs to you when he has relationship disputes because he knows you will always side with him. If a mother can objectively guide her son to handle a dispute, she is helping him. If she only sees his conflict through his eyes she is hindering him. If you are going to intervene, support him when he is right but push your emotional attachment aside and challenge him when he is wrong.

When you bail him out of trouble and don't hold him accountable for his actions, you're not challenging or teaching him to properly handle his own conflict. It is not your job to rescue him, but every time you do, you become his crutch. When he doesn't operate responsibly, consequences will teach him. If he forgets to pay his electricity bill and the power is cut off, he will learn from that situation if you don't bail him out. If he pays for concert tickets with the money he needs for bills, don't help him with his bills. He will learn from that experience when he's eating dinner in the dark. He will understand that the concert shouldn't have been a priority over his light bill.

You carried him for nine months and then two to three years after he was born. You have carried him long enough. Teach him to walk on his own two feet. Statistics show the attachment for mothers to sons is higher than mothers to daughters. Also, it starts early in his adolescent years. It starts with you being overbearing anytime someone gets near him or you overreacting when he falls and hurts himself. You're not allowing him the opportunity to grow and do things on his own terms by learning how to fall, get hurt and get up on his own. He needs to be able to listen to his own instinct regarding danger. When he gets too close to the edge of a porch step, instead of yelling and frantically pulling him away, hold his hand and let him see how it feels to be close. Trust me, he will only get so close before he turns back to you. Navigating dangerous situations without angst is a learned skill that moms too often deprive their young sons of.

For example, at 5 years old, a son drops a toy and his mother picks it up instead of allowing him to pick it up himself. At 8, he falls while trying to learn to ride his bike and she is too scared to let him get back on the bike to try again. Now he is 15 years old and just learning to ride a bike when he should be preparing to learn to drive a car. Falling is a necessary part of the process of learning. If you allow him to fall, he will pick himself up, dust himself off and try it again until he gets it right.

If he drops something on the floor, make him pick it up. If he throws something out of anger, make him go pick it up. Starting young will teach him to choose another way and it will help him to learn respect at a young age. Make him clean up his mess when he eats or has a snack, even if when he is young and requires more assistance. If he steps out of line, don't allow him to talk back to you after you have issued your directive. Hold him accountable and take away his privileges including his video games, live sporting events, or time playing outside.

I witnessed a little boy around the age of 3 or 4 cursing at his mother. She told her girlfriends that she thought it was cute. It wasn't cute; it was disrespectful to say the least and he should have been disciplined. My mom would have knocked me out. Allowing or encouraging any of this behavior from a young age creates a rude grown boy who continues the same behavior that once seemed cute but now sounds hurtful and offensive as he stands taller, and his voice is deeper and sounds more like that of a man.

Doing his homework, shopping for him without his assistance, lying for him or cleaning his room will not prepare him to understand the importance of accountability, integrity, obedience and self-sufficiency. By the age of 12, he should be doing these things for himself or with your assistance. If he is a teenager and doesn't know how to fry or boil an egg, doesn't know how to turn on the stove, doesn't know how to find bread, turkey, lettuce and tomato to fix his own sandwich, you are failing to equip him with basic skills. When he says he likes the way you make his sandwich and cut it down the middle and you fall for it every time, stop it! You are not letting him grow up.

Teach Self-Sufficiency

You can help improve your son's mindset by teaching him to be self-sufficient from a young age. When the day comes for him to put his own key into his apartment or house door and make his own decisions, you want him to be ready. When he is ready to choose his mate, you want him to be emotionally astute, able to capably communicate and be economically able to provide for himself and his significant other. There's nothing wrong with your son coming back to ask for advice, but the final decision should ultimately be his. If he makes a bad decision, don't be so hard on him. He will learn from his mistakes.

Don't let your anxiety trick you into thinking that the task will not be accomplished unless you do it for him. When you allow him to take a nap while you are out there doing all the work, you are creating a lazy mama's boy. That mama's boy is going to meet a real woman who's looking for a real man and she's going to be turned off if his behavior is childlike. She's going to have an issue with him not making decisions on his own. Wouldn't you be turned off if you dated a man with those qualities?

Whether he's a baby or he reaches manhood and leaves your home, you always have an opportunity to teach him life skills. There is a good chance that you have a busy schedule and life is hectic, but if you take a few moments daily or weekly to teach him, he will get it. Give him the instructions. Sometimes you may need to repeat the instructions a few times; men have delayed hearing. After he hears your instruction, step back and allow him to figure it out and think for himself. Every time he gains an understanding of how to do something new, it will build him and it will free up more of your time. Trust that he will make the right decisions and believe that he can do it. Even if he gets it wrong once or twice, continue to encourage him and allow the process to work. One day you will be proud of the man you have raised.

What Your Son Should Know By Age 12

(Start enforcing these steps as early as 3 or 4 years of age)

By the Age of 12, Your son should be able to do the following:

- Make his bed, including changing his sheets
- Dress himself, including picking out his clothes, shoes, and belt. A bonus would be teaching him (or have someone teach him) how to tie a tie
- Assist you in shopping for his clothes
- Operate a stove, boil pasta, fry or boil an egg, make his own sandwich, cut up fruit
- Bathe, wash his face, clean his body, put on deodorant,

brush his teeth and floss, and lotion his body

- Do his homework with minimal help
- Have a weekly/daily chore (e.g.: taking out the trash, washing dishes, or straightening the living room)
- Be respectful to others and himself
- Understand the importance of hard work. (Proper preparation prevents poor performance)
- Understand that when he makes bad decisions, there are consequences

Ensure Your Son Stands on His Own

To ensure your son stands on his own and does not rely on you, speak positive words into his life daily. Be the example that you want to see in him by living by faith, not fear. Trust that your son will make the right decisions based on your teaching and upbringing. If he works hard, he will reap the benefits of his time and sacrifice. If he slacks and does things with a lazy attitude, it will be tougher to achieve his goals. If he becomes indifferent about his life. He will find himself lost and unable to progress.

Teach him that if he makes bad decisions, there are consequences. Hold him accountable for his actions. Let him know that his choices, not his color, will define his future. I always share with the young men I mentor that I have never seen an eagle fly with a chicken. Eagles (people with a growth mindset) fly high and chickens (people who live in fear or make bad choices) can't reach those heights. I believe that if you show me your friends, I'll show you your future. Your son must choose his friends wisely. Some of his old friends may not be capable of going where his ability will take him; that's okay.

I have not met an adult who hasn't made at least one bad decision, but bad decisions are not always negative. Don't baby and pamper your son when he fails at something. Mothers, sometimes the anxiety that you feel and create when your son is hurt is worse than your son hurting himself. Properly handled, bad decisions can help your son grow. Teach him to find the lesson in his mistakes and to try again with assurance in his newfound understanding.

Also, allow him to move outside of his comfort zone. He may feel uncomfortable if he is pushed beyond his limited experiences. This is not always a bad thing; it places him in the position to view life through a different perspective, to find out that he is capable of achieving more than the thought. Being uncomfortable can sometimes produce a "sink or swim" attitude. If you don't develop for the better, you will stay stagnant or regress.

Guide him to move forward with intention, making individual decisions that are good for him. When he reaches a certain age, you can get help from a mentor outside of your home, whether it's a counselor, pastor, coach, teacher, etc. A mentor will be a needed fresh voice to reiterate what you have taught him, maybe from a different perspective. Also, a mentor may be able to teach him things that you can't or didn't think of.

Instill confidence and teach him how to affirm himself. Affirm him if he does something good. Instruct and encourage him to make wiser choices when he doesn't do well. Build his confidence and character by coaching him to learn on his own, giving him the opportunity to figure it out. Mothers, don't be so hard on yourself. If you have been treating your son like a mama's boy, pivot and change the behavior. Don't look back because you can't do anything about what's already done. You can't fix the past, but a little patience and guidance can change your son's future for the better.

You Can't Be Both

Some mothers try to be both mother and a father to their sons. This is understandable, especially when a mother sees the pain their son experiences when his father is not present. In these situations, mothers feel like they must play a dual role in raising their children. Whether you feel this way or not, you're not his father. You are only his mother.

On top of inherited traits and personality types, a lot of people grow up in some kind of family dysfunction. Twenty-five to thirty percent of children from birth to four years of age have already experienced an episode of trauma. Over 50% of people walking around today have experienced trauma in their lives on more than one occasion. When young men carry this trauma, it is exasperated when their father is absent. A father's absence, or a father who is there physically but absent emotionally or psychologically, triggers a traumatic response. What your son grows up with is his environment. It is hereditary. How society responds to his heredity is key to how he will be perceived. In this instance I'm referring to environment as his father being absent or him not having a whole mother because she has been broken by her own circumstances. When the mother attempts to become both the son's mother and father, he is confused. I have heard mothers even say the phrase, "I'm your mother and your father." Saying it or thinking that it's true doesn't make you his mother and father. When it comes from a place of hurt and anger, or even when it comes from a place of love, it doesn't change the fact that you can only ever be your son's mother.

Some mothers grow up hearing this from their own mother, and eventually it becomes a mantra that has become embedded into their spirit. When things don't work out with them and their son's father or they feel like they are the only one putting in effort to raise their son, maybe they repeated the same mantra that they heard from their mother and/or grandmother. The phrase becomes comfortable to say, particularly when a father doesn't live in the house, or doesn't have a good relationship with her. Sometimes the phrase is said when the father is a lousy husband but is trying to be present in the lives of his children. The father could have been one of the worst husbands ever, but he may be paying child support and spending time with his children even though he's not living in the home. The fact that he was a lousy husband or boyfriend doesn't mean he is not a good father.

A mother cannot take a father's place and a father cannot take a mother's place. Some stores sell greeting cards and postcards for mothers on Father's Day, and in random homes women are celebrated as "fathers" on this day. This confusion is out of control. Even if the movement is meant to praise mothers for their diligence with their sons, it causes "super" moms and their children to shut out those fathers who didn't work out with the mother but may want to be in their sons' lives. A failed relationship doesn't necessarily have to correlate to an absent father. In the cases when the father wants to be present, some mothers who attempt to be both shut fathers out. When the mother is in her emotions about their failed relationship and attempts to take on both roles, while preventing him from being there for their son, she does more damage than good. It damages the potential relationship between father and son. It prevents the father from playing his role and it prevents the son from benefitting from having him there. If you had a horrible break-up or divorce, don't let it stop invested fathers from being in their kids' lives.

The benefits of sons having their fathers in their lives includes increased self-esteem. According to the American Academy of Pediatrics, when fathers are involved, it promotes inner growth and strength. When fathers are involved, their children tend to not only do better in school but stay out of trouble. A son's mental and social development is improved when he has the support of his father.

Don't Block His Father's Efforts

If your son doesn't have his father in his life, don't overcompensate by trying to make up for a father's absence or negligence. When he is lacking something at home, overcompensating is the worst thing you can do. Being overbearing won't help either; in fact, it will push him away. A young man loves his father deep down inside, even if he's never met him. Your son wants to know where he comes from, and, in the case of an absent father, he wants answers to why his father is not in his life. Deep down a son could even feel like it's his fault that his father doesn't come around. Reassure him that is not the case; that he did nothing wrong. Remind him that his father is dealing with his own issues.

If his father is in jail, for example, he is there due to circumstances not pertaining to him. If his father has remarried and chose not to be active in his son's life, it is due to the father's lack of parental accountability. If your son's father has been abusive toward you and/or your son, and you feel safer with him not having access, explain to your son why your choice to keep his father away is in his best interest at that time. If you ignore or lie to your son, he will harbor resentment toward you.

Regardless of the reason that his father is not around, get your son involved with good men in his life. The father could have passed away or he could be a deadbeat, but you chose this person to be your son's father. I know sometimes you question that decision, but the reality is: he is the father. However, there are good men out there who play an important role in saving our young men. Whether at church, at a community center, or sporting event, get your son involved with good men who can mentor and guide him along with your guidance.

When your sons' friends have their dads in their lives, it's a good idea to expose him to his friends with dads so he can see the intended interaction between a man and young man. Fathers and sons have trials and tribulations just like anyone else, and your son will understand the importance of that bond while seeing the good and bad of their relationship. Not to mention he may gain a mentor out of the relationship.

Build a Support Team of Good Men and Women around Your Son

Being a mother is a long-term, ongoing commitment. It is okay to seek help raising your son. There is no shame in getting capable assistance. As a matter of fact, creating a support team around you and your son will better ensure a successful turnout for his future. Start early. Surround him with good men and women, from coaches to the right school counselors, teachers, heads of community organizations, church members and community leaders. Ask pertinent questions about opportunities available for your son. Take your time and find the right fit and don't be afraid of removing people from his life who are not giving him the proper guidance.

When I was seven years old, I wasn't old enough to join Wheelers Boys Club in Indianapolis, which was in the inner city, but my mom was aggressive in her pursuit to surround me with good men. When she took me to be enrolled, she rolled the dice knowing that there was a chance I wouldn't be accepted because I was too young. Despite the odds being against me, she was on a mission. That day, I met a man who would change my life forever and became one of my lifetime mentors. His name was Dr. Ralph Dowe. He knew right off that I wasn't old enough to be there (you had to be 9 years old to join). Dr. Dowe asked my mother, "How old is your son?"

At first my mom lied and said I was nine, then she told the truth. She said, "He is seven years old, but he really needs positive male role models in his life, and this would be a good place for him. I have nowhere else to turn." She seriously wanted me in the Boys Club because in her mind it would be a good place for me to go after school to keep me out of trouble.

Ralph chuckled and said, "I appreciate your aggressiveness."

He allowed me to join Wheelers Boys Club in Indianapolis. My mom thanked him for giving me a safe alternative to the streets and especially for making an exception for my age.

Mom, you must have this same sense of urgency early in your son's life. Don't wait until life and the world gets hold of him. Every person, young and old, needs a mentor. As a member of the Wheelers Boys Club of Indianapolis, I later became academic member of the year, Youth of the Year for Indianapolis and State Youth of the Year for Indiana my senior year of high school. As a matter of fact, I took my first trip on an airplane because I was a member of that club. Ralph Dowe's mentorship and encouragement saved my life.

Even as your son gets older, it would be advantageous for you to consider the areas that will be helpful to your son, that you can't afford, have no interest in or knowledge of, and find mentors that can fill those roles. For example, if your son is into sports, help him find a mentor who enjoys going to sporting events and doesn't mind taking your son along with him. If your son needs help with Math or English, help him find a tutor that will be able to give him a better understanding than his teacher. If your son is interested in Financial Literacy, help him find a mentor who can teach him how to save, invest and grow money. The options are endless and there is always a well-intentioned adult who would be willing to share their knowledge with your son. You simply have to put forth the effort to find them.

Find Programs in Your Area

There should be numerous enrichment programs available in your area or online. You can sign your son up in order to help him achieve the goals that he may have for himself. Many are free, while some may require an investment. An investment in programming for your son will benefit him more than a high-priced material item like a video game or overpriced sneakers. Take the time to research programs that are available to meet your son's needs. It will be well worth it. Also, be sure to get your son involved early and often.

Every young man will not excel in school sports and that's okay. If your son doesn't, this means you must expose him to other activities that may catch his attention. He can learn how to play an instrument or participate in other extracurriculars such as Tae Kwon Do, which teaches discipline and accountability. He could find an interest in acting, playing chess, coding/game programming, mentoring, choir/singing, dancing, writing, or student government. Investigate and find positive programs that work for both of your schedules and his personality.

Encouraging your son to be involved in activities will free you up to do other things for yourself. Don't give up when one program doesn't pan out. Go find another one. Have faith and move forward. The first program my mother signed me up for was the Big Brothers program. I was on the waiting list my whole childhood and never received a call to be matched up with a Big Brother. The wait was frustrating and hurtful, but my mom was proactive and didn't give up. She continued her search for a positive program until she found one that met my needs.

It is important that you understand the value of your son's learning from the right men and women through mentorship, community, and school programs. Being involved in this way will allow others to push your son and give him good insight. If the program is positive, sign him up immediately. If the mentor is capable, allow him or her to invest in your son with your blessing.

According to Harvey Robbins, author of *How to Speak and Listen Effectively*, "Effective communication exists between two people when the listener interprets the speaker's message the way the speaker intended. An interpersonal communication gap occurs when the meaning of a message is interpreted and reacted to in a manner different from what was intended." Your communication style may be altogether different from your son's and that's okay. There is an age gap that, in most cases, causes a cultural gap. Kids today communicate via text message and social media, and they tend not to make eye contact when speaking with others face-to-face. Parents also text and use social media, but depending on what age, most parents will pick up the phone and engage in conversation. You must find a communication style that works for you and your son so that you both can have a better way to exchange and receive information.

Six Techniques That Help Improve Communication

Robbins offers six techniques to improve communication. These techniques could be used as tools when communicating with your son. The goal here is using the techniques to help you find a style of communicating that is most effective for both you and your son. This takes practice and patience. It is important when relating to your son that you see him as a human being to be understood and guided and not to be controlled. Also, misunderstandings happen during communication, but the following tools will help you to regain and keep your exchanges with your son on track:

1. **Use Feedback.** Ask your son what he thinks about your communication style. Does he receive the information effectively? If not, find out specifically what is not working and deliberately work to change your style. If you yell too much, work to bring down your tone. If you are quick to respond, slow down and work to listen more. If you condemn your son for wrongdoing before you get a clear explanation of the situation, give him a chance to share with you his side of the story, listening closely to the details before rushing to judgement.

2. **Use Multiple Channels.** Work together with your son to determine the best way to communicate in any given situation. You may find that there is no one solution. For quick chats and reminders, texting

may be easier. To share funny or informative content, social media is the way to go (e.g., TikTok, Snapchat or Instagram). If something needs to be communicated during school hours, you may need to send an email or text. If it is of a more serious nature, a call may be the best way to contact your son. Establish with him that you will not blow up his phone, calling continuously if he agrees to text you if he is unavailable to pick up the phone.

3. **Be Sensitive to the Receiver.** If your son does not receive your instruction in the midst of a disagreement or during simple conversations, your delivery may be undesirable. You will know because he will not respond effectively. His body language and response to what you are saying will let you know how receptive he is being. If you feel resistance, be aware that you may have said something that may have tapped into emotions linked to a previous incident, past pain or negative feelings. Belittling comments, snide remarks and unfair blame can cause your son to respond with out-of-control emotions. Understand that he is reacting. If he lashes out at you, instead of lashing back, take a deep breath, compose your own emotions, and ask him to explain why what you said sent him into a tailspin. Actively listen. If he describes your approach as over the top, judgmental, or critical, apologize and let your son

know that you didn't mean to push his buttons. Encourage him to apologize for his reaction, then move forward. Changing your approach doesn't mean that you don't hold your son accountable. The message is the same despite the delivery, however it is generally better received when you are more composed. You don't have to use such a forceful or overblown delivery to be heard. Once control is established with both you and your son, always get back to the root of the issue at hand to find solutions.

4. **Be Aware of Symbolic Meanings.** Symbolic meanings include gestures, body language, facial expressions, and verbal emissions. Observe your son when he walks in the door, and you will have a pretty good idea of how his day went even before he tells you. Adjust your approach accordingly. Energy is important. Always try to be upbeat and fun. At times you may need to speak with a sympathetic tone. He may need a moment to clear his head before you bombard him with questions. Give him that time. Whatever the case may be, reading the symbolic meaning of your son's body language will allow you to properly respond.

5. **Use Simple Language.** Use basic language that your son understands. If you use words that are difficult to understand and your son seems unclear

of a definition, take the time to define the word for your son. Just make sure you are not talking over his head. Use language that is simple and relatable.

6. **Use Repetition.** It's okay to repeat yourself or reiterate your message to make sure your son receives it. If he doesn't understand, take the time to define what you are relaying to him. We all forget things, so repetition is important. Reminders may be annoying, but they are necessary. Most of us hear our mother or grandmother's voice in the back of our mind, "Don't sit your drink down and go back to it," or "Take someone with you when you go to strange places" or "Give it to God and let it go." We all could use more reminders about the right things to do because we often forget.

Confront Little Things Before an Explosion Occurs

Explosions don't just happen. They result from a series of stressful events that causes intense emotional pressure to build within an individual. A warehouse can catch fire and may burn for a period. If the fire department pulls up and puts out the fire, the building can be saved with little damage, depending on how quickly firefighters arrive. On the other hand, if that fire continues to burn and someone walks by and throws cans filled with gasoline into the warehouse, the gas will accelerate the fire, and could cause an explosion. Similarly, if you continue to provoke your son, he will explode. At some point he will no longer be able to control his emotions. Some moms constantly physically abuse their sons, slapping them for making bad grades, for not properly caring for their younger siblings, for not playing well in a sporting event, for forgetting to complete a chore, or other minor offenses. Other mothers verbally abuse their sons, ridiculing them when they make a mistake or calling them degrading names like, "punk," "pussy," or "wimp." Consistent abrasive and thoughtless behavior toward your son is bound to cause an explosion.

To prevent this from happening, be proactive instead of reactive. If you see your son slacking in a certain area, address it right away with love and instruction rather than stress, strife and yelling. If your son makes a bad grade, have a discussion with him about his interaction with the teacher and probe by asking questions like, "Are you having trouble comprehending this subject?" or "Do you need a tutor?" You may find that he needs a little more assistance in that subject and that's okay. We have all needed help in classes. If your son doesn't play well in a sporting event, he may be having an off night. After speaking with him, you may find that he was dealing with something outside of the sport that affected his play. You also may want to examine yourself. Maybe you want him to be successful in the sport for your own self-gratification and bragging purposes, but sports may not be for him. If he forgets to do a chore, it is not the end of the world. Give him the opportunity to get it right. Also remember that even you have forgotten to do things at times. How would you want to be treated if you forgot something? You would want another chance.

Likewise, don't allow your son's behavior to cause you to lose control of your emotions. It's tough when you feel disrespected, however, it is important to keep your emotions intact. Give yourself time to stop and analyze the situation before making harsh comments or acting irrationally. Work to not take his mishaps so personally. Holding on to stress causes diseases and sickness, so don't hold grudges or keep score. Everybody makes bad decisions, and your son is no different, and neither are you.

As he grows into a teenager and deals with his hormones, he may respond to you with an attitude instead of kind words. It has nothing to do with you, so don't take it personally. He is trying to master his own emotions. Give him time to figure them out. Remember, the earlier you instruct him on how he should address you, the better the chance that he will default to a more respectful way of speaking to you as he gets older.

Men often suppress their issues, so don't expect your son to open up to you without any reservations. Sometimes boys alienate themselves when they have problems. Build trust with him. Let him know your "door is always open" if he needs to talk. If you don't feel like he will come to you, provide him with someone else to confide in when he needs advice or a listening ear. If you are aware of a particular issue that he is dealing with and you have had experience with the issue, let him know that you were once young and you understand what he is dealing with. Discuss with him how you worked through it or the pitfalls you experienced if you didn't handle it properly. Either way, being transparent with your son will go a long way in helping him to handle his own situation.

Daily Positive Affirmations for Your Son

Teach your son to affirm himself by having him repeat these statements daily:

1. I am a man of God
2. I am smart
3. I am equipped to walk in my calling
4. I love myself
5. I enjoy learning
6. I love my siblings
7. I value the importance of keeping my room clean
8. I am respectful to others
9. I do my best daily
10. I value peace and my actions reflect that
11. I control my emotions and remain calm

Have your son repeat positive affirmations every day until they become a part of his daily dialogue. These are not words that should be spoken just when he feels like it. Saying them is just as important as him washing his face and brushing his teeth every morning. It's like planting a seed; you must fertilize the soil for years to ensure proper growth. Then you put the seed into the ground and water it until it grows into a plant. Same with your son. Deposit positive words into your son's heart daily and allow him to begin the growth process. Affirming him early and often is important because, just like the seed needs to be nurtured to grow, your son needs to be nurtured and prepared to face the elements of life that could endanger him as he matures into his manhood.

The elements include his peers at school and in his community. He will be ready for whatever they say to and about him and he can react appropriately because of his daily affirmations. He may be called derogatory names. He might be told that he's not worth anything. There is a possibility that he may hear that he's not smart. He may even be told that guys that look like him do not become successful (as I was once told). Some statistics will lead him to believe he is supposed to be dead or in jail. Remind him that he is the righteousness of God and he is not a mistake. Remind him that he can conquer anything he sets his mind to.

If you consistently affirm him and teach him to affirm himself from the time he is young, he is more likely to be prepared to reject negative comments that come his way. You will have already planted the seeds of self-confidence, self-determination and self-respect. You will have already told him that he's great, that he's smart, that he can conquer the world. So why would he not believe those things for himself? Have him repeat those phrases daily to remind him of who he is. If he says it enough, he will eventually start believing it because words are powerful! Words create! Positive words build self-esteem!

As you affirm your son, remember to speak positive truths about yourself. Tell yourself that you can do all things. Tell yourself that you are healed. Tell yourself that, despite the circumstances, you are worthy to be happy and you can move forward from past pain. No matter what you have been through in your life, you can always change your direction with work and determination. God is not through with you. Tell yourself that you are calm and will not let anyone compromise your peace. Write five to six positive words or phrases about yourself. Repeat them daily because your positive energy and peace will spread from you to your son.

Respect Your Son's Voice

Respecting your son's opinions and thoughts starts with being a respectful listener. You gain an understanding of a person's desires by listening. Your son's voice deserves to be heard. By doing so, you gain valuable information about him. If he doesn't feel heard and shuts down, it will be hard for him to open back up again. As a child, you may have been told to be quiet, shut up or go to another room when adults were speaking. This is a bad habit that a lot of adults have because it has been passed down from generation to generation. When your parents said something, you may not have been given the opportunity to voice your thoughts. Think about how limiting that was for you. Your son may have something valuable to add to the conversation. Allow him to chime in on select topics and discussions.

He should be able to express his feelings freely and without fear of being judged. By doing so, he will learn good communication skills. Let him finish his statements without being cut off so he can know that his thoughts and opinions are valid and valued. Guided and open-minded conversations can lead to him learning problem solving, creative thinking, and leadership skills.

A lot of young men are not comfortable speaking with adults, including their parents. Encourage your son that speaking about his feelings and emotions also brings healing. If your son walks around the house not saying anything, that could be a sign that he has shut down and feels his voice isn't being heard.

If your son says something that's out of the ordinary or derogatory, address it but still hear him out. He is your son. Spending time with him will bring trust and strength to your relationship. If his emotions are out of control, teach him a respectful way of handling them without yelling, screaming, or losing your temper. Giving your son a voice means responding calmly after hearing something that might make you uncomfortable.

Cut the Umbilical Cord

When a baby is born, the umbilical cord connecting the baby to the mother's placenta is cut to prevent health issues like blood cancer, clots or respiratory issues. Similarly, there is an invisible emotional umbilical cord that connects mothers to their children after birth. At some point in your son's life, it needs to be cut. It's really not that hard, unless you are living in fear. When you let go, you will allow him to experience his own life lessons, which he must learn for himself. These lessons are necessary for his own personal growth. Don't be afraid or angry when he decides to move out of your house. Don't talk him out of moving to the next city or across the country. Try to look at the benefits of him moving like him making his own decisions for once or you gaining a new place to visit.

If he lives nearby, he may continue to come to your house to eat. He might ask you to do his laundry if you let him. He shouldn't be allowed to just show up at your house anytime. The key you gave him should be used only for emergencies. As much as you may enjoy his company, you have to set visitation limitations for his own good and yours. As much as you may enjoy cooking for him and doing his laundry, it is imperative that you teach him to be self-sufficient. As the saying goes, "Give a man a fish and he will eat for a day. If you teach that man how to fish, he will eat for a lifetime." Practice this even before he leaves your home.

Stop saying, "He's my baby and will be my baby forever," because he really will remain a baby under this mindset. See your grown son as a man. If your son is legally an adult but has no discipline, this means you raised him with little to no accountability. It's hard to go back and try to teach when he is an adult. However, if you dropped the ball, don't get down on yourself; remember that life will teach him all he needs to know. The best thing that you can do is to be honest and let him know that you didn't always know the right things to teach him, but that you believe in him and you did your best. Then show him by encouraging him to be better and to do better despite anything he may not have received from you growing up. This is a humbling, yet effective position from which to relate to your son.

When Mothers Have Negative Habits but Expect Different Results in their Sons

How do you interact with others? What does your son hear come out of your mouth when you are angry? How do you handle conflict? The way that you handle the details of communicating in your daily life, including how you interact with people both inside and outside of your home, can create negative behavior within your children. If you are at home on the phone with your girlfriend, calling her the “b” word or “h” word, or other disrespectful names, you are influencing your son. Like a sponge, he soaks up your conversations as he listens to all the disrespect you spew, even when you’re joking. The last thing your son needs to see is his mother reveling in negative acts. For him, perception becomes reality. When he hears cursing and yelling regularly, it becomes an acceptable form of communication to him. There is nothing shocking about it to his ear. It becomes a norm.

When disciplining your child, if you yell and scream at him, you are not teaching. You are fussing at him, showing that you are anxious and agitated by what he did. When there is no clear intention behind a rant, it is not discipline. Effective discipline is done by having an honest conversation pointing out the bad behavior. Then you give your child the opportunity to explain his actions. Once that is settled, clearly state what the consequences are. Have him apologize and then discuss with your son a better choice that could have been made to prevent him from landing in trouble. All this needs to be done with love and care with the goal that your son learns something from the incident. Little to no screaming or yelling is necessary. With practice, you might be able stay calm despite the circumstance.

When you scold him for something he did wrong, if your child walks away from you feeling hurt, misunderstood, and unheard, there's a good chance he hasn't learned anything. If he changes his behavior, it may be out of fear and not out of understanding. Operating out of fear causes resentment and misdirection.

As a middle and high school educator, it amazed me when young men entered my classroom cursing and being disrespectful. But when I met their moms, I immediately knew where the behavior originated. In fact, some of the moms were worse than their sons, coming into our meeting talking loudly and being disrespectful before the conversation had a chance to begin. Even though some of the young men were just as disrespectful as their mothers, they seemed to be embarrassed when they witnessed their moms behave in a similar way. Mothers, your actions and words have influence over your sons.

If a son is being negatively influenced at home, school and from others in his neighborhood, he will carry that inappropriateness to church members, teachers, coaches and his peers. Children learn negative behavior from others, whether it's other children or adults in their surroundings. Don't get upset with the schools for kicking him out for his disrespectful behavior. Realize that he may have learned it from you or his environment. Nonetheless, he must be held accountable for his actions. As his parent, you must be held accountable for your actions. After all, negative behavior doesn't fall out of the sky; it's taught.

Some people behave negatively as a result of brokenness. Brokenness means having been fractured or to no longer be in one piece or working order. Everyone is flawed, but to be broken is not healthy. It is a state of mind that must be healed in order to have healthy relationships. Most people act out what they learned from negative parents, family members and friends. If negativity is all you have been around your whole life, you may not understand anything different because you weren't exposed to enough positive healthy relationships and communication. It's easy to become unmoved by negativity in your life. But if you are honest with yourself, there is a residue of pain lingering from the negative relationships from your past. The pain you feel is real, but it doesn't have to last.

Pain is addressed by healing, understanding and breaking old habits. Healing is a choice, and you must seek and choose it for yourself. The adversary works overtime to keep you stressed out and living in pain. Pain influences bad choices. If your mind is occupied with pain, it is tough for you to manifest love. It becomes more difficult to find joy in everyday life. It seems impossible to be at peace. Living in past pain and negativity keeps you stuck in a pattern of negativity, including negative thoughts and negative actions.

STEPS IN THE HEALING PROCESS

Positive words stop negative thoughts. Use your words to speak out against evil, pain and negativity.

1. Admit that you are hurt, write down the details of your pain to release it from your spirit.

2. Speak to someone who you trust and who will give you good advice and guidance (sometimes that person is not your friend).

3. Forgive those who have hurt you. Understand that forgiving is not for the other person, but for your well-being.

4. Practice healing the trauma and past pain that you have experienced in your life and teach your child to do so as well.

The key to changing the negative behavior is controlling your emotions. In the face of your emotions, it is important to control your responses and how you handle conflict. Control the words that come out of your mouth and don't let your anger get the best of you. This can be difficult to do when other people's actions push your buttons, bringing to the surface unresolved pain. Your goal in changing negative behavior is to tap into your past pain and work to heal from the things that you cannot change. Speak to someone about your hurts so that you can heal and move forward. Find ways to practice self-care, including prayer, meditation, exercise and other relaxation methods. As you get in touch with your calmer, more relaxed side, you will be able to better see your toxic side and work to change the unwarranted behaviors.

You don't want to pass your hurt on to your children. It happens all too often. As you heal, you can help your child heal. When healing takes place, you can move toward more respectful communication. Just like toxic behavior is taught, respect is taught. If you want your son to grow up to be respectful, model to him what respect looks like. In most cases, he will follow your example.

Monitor Your Communication

You are the very first woman your son will encounter. He will compare every woman he meets to you. Take that seriously. When facing obstacles or confronting difficult circumstances in life, you don't have to be loud to be heard. If you are frequently addressing your girlfriends as bitches and whores and laughing about it, you are not being respectful with your words. Being unruly or irrational is not the only way to be heard. If your circle of friends thrives on dramatic, offensive interactions to be seen and heard, maybe you should keep those interactions away from your son. Or better yet, consider spending more time with a circle of friends who respects each other's voices, opinions and children.

Be an Effective Listener

Listening to your son could be life or death for him. Many kids fight depression and anxiety, which could lead to suicide. Everyone has a need to be loved and to share love, to be understood and to feel needed and wanted. Listening is a big part of this.

A good listener seeks to gain an understanding of what the other person says and means. This means that you must actively listen with no intention of interjecting or trying to prepare what you are going to say before the speaker can even get his point across. It's challenging to listen and talk at the same time. Many people are poor listeners, especially when listening only with the intent of responding. Good listening skills improve communication and help you understand the person you're speaking with.

According to Robbins, "Immediately following a speech, the average listener has comprehended approximately 50 percent of what he or she heard and within 48 hours, the comprehension level has dropped to 25 percent or less." This means that people rarely retain what they hear and as time goes by we lose the information we thought we heard.

When you are conversing with your son, don't hijack the conversation or cut him off to make your point when he has the floor. If you're like me and have trouble retaining information, sometimes you might have to take notes so you can reference what you heard. After he speaks, repeat a few of his comments so he knows that you were listening. If you don't have an understanding of what he said, ask him to clarify. Then you can respond to him. You will not always agree, but you must respect his viewpoint understanding that we all see things differently. Sometimes you have to agree to disagree. Other times you may have to let him know that although you respect his point of view, it doesn't line up with the way you have chosen to keep your house and that as a member of your household, he has to follow your rules.

Sometimes sons just need you to listen and not try to fix the situation with words. If he trusts you, he will vent to you about a variety of subjects. Show him that you are actively listening by displaying good body language. Sit up straight and give good eye contact and nod from time to time to let him know you hear him. When engaging with your son, put away your cell phone, mute the TV, or pause anything that may distract you. Listening attentively helps to build a strong, healthy relationship with your son because he knows your focus in his time of need is solely on him.

Have you ever been in a situation where you were trying to get your point across, but you felt like the person you were speaking to was half listening or not listening at all? Did you become frustrated? If you have felt this way, you'd better believe that you son feels it from you when you don't prioritize his communication. To become a better listener, take a deep breath and intentionally hold any comments that you may have. Choose to hear what the other person has to say. Listening is a basic part of communication. Our parents teach us to speak, schools teach us to read and write. Listening is rarely taught in schools or homes. Nonetheless, everyone wants to feel heard. Work to become an active listener and be slow to respond. Your son will begin to mirror you and become a more active listener.

Establishing Respect in Your Household

Chapter 5

Many mothers are inundated with pain and sometimes don't realize how the turmoil from past experiences affects the decisions they make in their everyday lives. Also, when young mothers have children and then become the head of a household with little to no training, they are challenged with figuring out how to establish a system that fosters a healthy home. It is difficult to think about this necessary but often overlooked detail, especially when a mother is trying to maintain and survive with little income, little support and little direction. Nonetheless, it is crucial to properly set up a well-defined flow of interaction between yourself, your children, your friends and the man in your life.

Respecting Yourself

Self-love starts from within. It means that you care about both how you treat yourself and how others treat you. It is the regard for one's own well-being and happiness. Self-respect means having pride and confidence in yourself. When you have pride in yourself, you care about how you see yourself and you care about how other people address and treat you. You care about the way you present yourself. When you are confident, you believe that your presence should be valued. You don't have to be dramatic to gain respect. Your understanding of who you are demands it. When you respect yourself, it is evident in the way you dress, in the words that you allow to come out of your mouth, in the people that you choose to be in your lives and in the day-to-day choices that you make for your own well-being and the well-being of your family.

If you have a husband who has been on drugs for years and steals from your household, he is going to repeatedly steal from you and your children. Whether it is your car, your kids games, Christmas gifts or other valuables, the addiction to his habit supersedes his empathy for the cares of your household. If he stays gone for days binging on drugs, he is being disrespectful to you and your children. Don't reward him by turning a blind eye to his actions. If you allow him back in your home without him making drastic changes to his lifestyle, he will go out and do the same thing again. Things will not improve; they may even get worse. If his drug habit takes provision from your household and you decide to borrow money from others to maintain, you become a crutch for him. Your financial hardship will only grow, making a strenuous home life for you and your son. Neither of you deserve this.

It your boyfriend lives with you yet refuses to work or help you take care of the responsibilities of your household, he is a hinderance to your family's well-being. If you motivate yourself daily to get up early and work all day to make sure your family has food and the household bills get paid, yet he tells you he doesn't want to work for "the man" but hasn't come up with one alternative to bring in income to the household. He is a deadbeat, a timewaster, and worthless to the household. If he stays home all day not cooking, not taking out the trash, not picking the kids up from school, not attempting to connect with your children, not cleaning but has no problem eating up all your children's food and snacks, he is selfish and doesn't care about you or your children. If the couch is his rest haven to watch TV entertaining himself playing video games while waiting for you to come home to cook dinner for him, this habit will not magically change. If when you ask him about getting a job he retaliates with verbal and/or physical abuse, he has out-of-control emotions and will continue to spew them out on you and maybe even your children as long as you allow him to. If you accept this behavior, you are accepting an inferior status in your own home. Do not make excuses for a coward like him. Remember your son is watching all of this and soaking up the foul, snake-like behavior. Your son is negatively affected and potentially taking on the same derogatory traits that he observes in the man that you have chosen to be the primary role model in his life.

Where is the self-respect in this situation? What kind of message does this send to your son? In such circumstances, your son learns that drugs are more important than family and he learns that it's okay not to work for a living. He learns that it is okay to play video games or watch TV all day and be lazy.

He learns that it is alright for his mother, and eventually the woman in his life, to work her butt off then come home and cook dinner for him despite his irresponsible and lazy disposition.

If you jump in and out of relationships and have a trail of men coming in and out of your life and home, it is disrespectful and unstable for your son. As soon as he gets attached to one of the men, you are off to the next one. Flirting with different men in front of your son is disrespectful too. If you are being intimate with someone who only calls you late at night, never takes you out on a date or to dinner and never spends valuable time getting to know you, you're not allowing yourself to be respected and you are disrespecting yourself. Late night visits from a man who claims to be interested in you is called a "Booty Call" amongst some men and women. If that's what you want, don't get in your feelings when that is how you are treated. My prayer is that you want more out of life than this. Men who are serious about getting to know you will call you in the middle of the day or early evening. They will take you on a date to lunch or dinner. They will want to be seen with you. Too many women, as my grandmother and aunt used to say, "Give up the milk for free."

When you settle for men who have no morals or values, you are degrading yourself. These are the same losers who will treat you and your kids badly. Most of the time they are takers, there for a free meal and whatever else they can get without working for it. Some of the men you have introduced to your son showed who they were from the beginning and you ignored it. These men rarely have anything nice to say to your son and often speak negatively about you and other women. When a man mistreats you, no matter how hard you try to hide it, your son will know and be affected. Respecting yourself and your son requires that you at least attempt to properly evaluate the men that you choose to bring around your son.

Love yourself enough to walk away from a relationship where the man you're with doesn't respect you enough to do his part. This is a tough pill to swallow, especially when you've been dating a man who has been disrespectful to you for five, ten, or twenty years. Your son is waiting for you to respect yourself enough to end the relationship. Ending that relationship will remind him that being in a woman's life is a privilege and not a right.

Growing up, I watched my stepfather mistreat my mom for years. My disgust for him grew like a wildfire. He walked around my house not speaking to me for weeks and months at a time. I didn't understand why my mom was with a man who disrespected her and me. When I was ten years old, he physically assaulted my mom and me. On another occasion on his birthday, he chose to hang out with his cousin rather than spend the evening with my mother. When he returned to the house early the next morning, he and my mother got into an argument. Fed up with my stepfather's disrespect, I inserted myself into the argument and tried to protect my mother, but he punched me in the face. His presence in our household for all those years inflicted mental, physical, and emotional pain that lasted for many years. You can prevent your son from experiencing this kind of turmoil by respecting and loving yourself enough to walk away from a toxic relationship.

How to Present Yourself

There is nothing on this Earth more precious than a woman. You were created in God's image and in my humble opinion made perfect, even with your imperfections. Yet, there is so much pressure on women to fit into society's view of an ideal woman. The world tells you how to wear your makeup, your hair, your eye lashes, your clothes, etc. Not that there is a problem with wearing any of that. If you like it, I love it. Just don't lose yourself while trying to become what you think someone else wants you to be.

I believe women are perfect the way they are. There is so much pressure on women to look like what they see in magazines and in the media. Many women fall victim to trying to fit these stereotypes. Over-the-top airbrushed depictions of women damage the mindsets of on-looking impressionable females young and old. They feel like they must assimilate to societal norms.

However, you must find a way to be comfortable with you. God created each of you with your own unique features. He created your curves, your long and short legs, your full bodies, your breasts. He created your lips, eye color, skin tone, etc. You were made an original. Be you. Society's ever-changing definition of beauty pressures women. Therefore, too many women get one surgery after another attempting to fit the mold, distorting their faces and bodies unnecessarily. Love yourself enough to work with what you have been given. Trust that you are enough.

If you don't love yourself, you will do things to disrespect yourself. Your son watches women disrespect themselves at his school, in his neighborhood, on social media and TV. He also watches the disrespectful way some women interact with each other. He may think that what they say and wear are inappropriate, but if he witnesses you doing the same thing, his ability to look at you with a high regard becomes challenging. His witnessing your identity crisis may also prompt a shift in the way he views himself. He may begin to scrutinize the way he looks and dresses trying to live up to the unrealistic norms of society. For example, you support your son by attending his basketball game, but you are dressed like you're going to a night club rather than his school-related event. While he appreciates you being there, he must deal with the side comments, frustration and embarrassment about what you are wearing. If you want your son to respect you, you must respect yourself by being more mindful of how you present yourself, not just to his friends and coaches but to others around you. Just like he represents you, you represent him.

Wearing skimpy clothing will not make men respect you. It might get their attention, but it will not make them want to build a meaningful relationship. No one is telling you to change who you are. Your style is your style. However, when you are going to a school function or a more family friendly event, it's okay to adjust your wardrobe to something more appropriate for the occasion.

Healthy Mother-Son Interaction

Your son should always address you with the utmost respect. You are his mom, not his friend and he should relate to you as such. Too many mothers are comfortable with their sons talking to them like they are their friends. This should be cautiously permitted. Your son should not be allowed to use foul language around you, talk back to you, raise his voice, talk over you, hang up on you, or speak to you in the same overused slang that he does with his friends. However, he should feel comfortable communicating to you about his hopes and dreams, situations that happened in each day, and instances with his friends while trusting that you will react in a way that allows him to feel safe and understood.

Buying him the new Jordans that just came out shouldn't be your way of gaining his approval and appreciation. Your focus shouldn't be on buying his happiness and affection. He will benefit more if you instead focus on preparing him to face life after he leaves your home. Reward him if he is doing well in school, being respectful and helping around the house. He shouldn't be rewarded with excessively expensive luxury items if he is not making good grades, respecting you as his mother and not doing his chores.

Teach Your Son Respect

Demand respect in your house by modeling it. Both respect and disrespect are taught. You are your child's first teacher and have the ability to show your son the value of respectful communication and the peace and rewards that come with it. Start when he is young. Even before he learns how to read, teach your son to value you and your instruction. If your son grows up listening to you curse him out, call him names, and tell him that he is stupid, he will learn disrespect from you. If you treat your son with disrespect first, don't expect a result other than disrespect from him. He will not value your instruction because you're reacting instead of teaching. If you feel upset, control your emotions, and teach him the importance and value of doing the same. Apologize when you lose your cool. Regroup and try your approach again.

If you are constantly calling the police on your son when you know you are the one who caused his trauma and pain in the first place, you are not respecting yourself or him. If you are running the streets going to the clubs Thursday through Sunday, coming in late and never spending quality time with your son, you are disrespecting yourself and him.

Relationally, you can disrespect yourself in the way you treat your son. Screaming at your son over minor offenses chips away at his self-esteem and self-worth. Over reacting aggressively toward your child for doing child-like things is another way you disrespect yourself by showing you have no control of your emotions. You disrespect yourself by not keeping your word and then getting upset when your son holds you accountable.

Even when you model correct behavior, your son will have his moments, but love conquers hate and strife every time. Consistency is the key, so don't give up. Be patient but diligent and understand that hard conversations take time and energy and can sometimes be painful. Keep working on creating a safe, peaceful environment in your home.

Teach Your Son to Respect Women

Mothers, teach your son to respect women. Show him how to treat you and if there is a man in your life, model positive interactions with him around your son. Teach him to open the door for you or his sisters. Have conversations with him about his day or the things happening in his life and let him know what's happening in yours so he can learn how to listen attentively to your thoughts. You are the first woman he will ever fall in love with. You are his model to not only understanding women but also to forming an opinion of how he will view, interact with, and emotionally connect to women. Be a positive example and equip him with the ability to properly regard you and women who will enter his life in the future. Your consistent behavior will teach him respect and will be just as powerful if not more so than your words.

Choose Friends Wisely

You may have one good friend in your lifetime because genuine people are hard to come across. If you have lived long enough, you may have already experienced betrayal from a so-called friend. Everyone doesn't have your best interest in mind. Some of your friends may have turned out to be jealous of you or you simply grew apart. Someone you grew up with may have remained immature. You may have had friends who changed, or you didn't see the value they were bringing to the table anymore. Maybe your friends no longer saw the value you were bringing to the table. Peaks and valleys exist in friendships.

Make it a point to discuss the character of the friends that your son chooses to allow into his circle. Make subtle suggestions about those who you don't feel are good choices, but ultimately allow him to make the final decision regarding his friends. Life will teach him and if the so-called friend lets him down, don't chastise. Just remind him that life is a journey of lessons and tell him to be sure to learn the lesson and to be more discerning about who he calls his friends.

My mom didn't allow all my friends into our home because she knew things that I didn't know and was able to see what I couldn't see. Her wisdom saved me a lot of grief. If she had an uneasy feeling about someone, they weren't allowed to come into our home. She was verbal about it in front of the person. She left nothing up to interpretation. I didn't understand at the time, but I grew to appreciate that about her. I thought she was being mean and abrasive at first. She regulated my friendships because she knew how influential my friends could be in my life. Be observant and pay attention to the group of people around your son.

While you can't choose all your son's friends, you can have some influence. Teach him to be around respectable young men who share his values, character, goals, dreams and work ethic. While he is still young, demonstrate what it means to be someone of good character and encourage him to be around people with the same energy.

Make the Most of Where You Live

Where you decide to live will have one of the biggest influences on your son's life because that is where he will meet most of his friends, gain his identity and begin to develop his goals for his future. It will also influence how he views life. Many mothers move into an area that isn't ideal simply because it is affordable. Understandably, parents sometimes end up in a neighborhood that doesn't encourage a healthy lifestyle and your sons suffer because of it. Regardless of whether you ended up in an unfavorable community due to divorce, job loss, or some other reason, know that your son will develop many of his habits from his surroundings.

The way I behaved as a young man was influenced by other young men that I grew up around. When I saw the older boys being disrespectful to each other and their parents, I found myself trying it out on my mother. It didn't end well, and I decided to let that habit go. My neighborhood affected me negatively in other ways as well. Experiencing the trauma and abuse of being bullied all the time caused me to be angry, frustrated and defensive even into my adult years. My neighborhood was violent, but that was the only place my mom could afford to live at the time. When we first moved in, she didn't even know it was a rough area. She had grown up in such a small shack in a rural town in Mississippi, that our house was a large step up in her eyes.

The teachings of my mother and coaches, community program involvement and watching the consequences of others' actions taught me one valuable lesson. I learned that living in a dangerous community didn't mean I had to succumb to the circumstances that surrounded me. Nonetheless, it wasn't an easy community to navigate. I needed a lot of guidance and support to not just get out alive but to not be manipulated into selling drugs, or fall victim to other traps in that environment. I had a few friends who were violent, but I also had friends who were non-violent; it was in my best interest to spend more time with them. As much as we tried to do the right thing and stay safe, two of my non-violent friends were murdered. It still hurts sometimes when I think about it. A person can be doing all the right things and still lose their life or end up in prison. Your surroundings matter! If you are in a negative atmosphere long enough, you will be exposed to negative elements and forced to deal with the repercussions that will affect you psychologically and emotionally.

If you're currently living in a community that is not the most ideal environment for your son, be proactive. Find programs run by trusted, credible organizations for him to join and stay busy.

As a result of joining good programs, I met positive friends from throughout the city, which gave me different perspectives. I was around other like-minded young men and young women who wanted to go to college and become successful. I met friends who desired to play college and pro sports like me. I met friends who took their education seriously. They made me feel comfortable being myself and not feeling guilty for being gifted and smart. Exposure to the right programs is a game-changer.

Preparing Your Son for the Different Stages of Manhood

When your son starts to crawl and then walk for the first time, he gets his first taste of freedom and independence. As trust is built, mothers allow their sons to walk freely but protect them from sharp edges around the house by padding them. You put up gates and block all stairs so that your child doesn't fall or tumble. Your baby has the freedom to roam around and find his way. As he gets older, you don't have to be as protective because he has better coordination and can maneuver around without falling as much, but he still needs guidance and support. Most moms are attentive and tend to properly guide their sons, knowing when to protect and when to stand back. Mothers, it is important to be just as attentive and supportive as he gets older, adjusting your efforts based on his stage in life.

When a young man is eight or nine years old, he sees himself as a big kid. His vocabulary improves greatly and he should be able to dress himself without your assistance. By the time your son moves into his tween years, he is teetering between childhood and adolescence. He'll want independence and privacy but will not be mature enough to make important decisions on his own. Even though you may see your son as independent and assume he can take on some of the adult responsibilities around the house, he is still just a kid. This is a time that he will need you more than ever. He is beginning to reach puberty. He is growing and changing. Your careful guidance, advice and love will help him tremendously during this time and prepare him to become a well-adjusted teenager.

When he becomes a teenager, he'll have growth spurts and deal with puberty changes, including facial and body hair, voice changes and his sexuality. Intellectually, he will be able to make plans and set short- and long-term goals. Emotionally, he will deal with peer pressure. This is a good time for you to help him develop his social skills and coach him on how to interact with others. If you prepare your son, he will perform well. Encourage him to take on new challenges. Help him to know, understand and appreciate who he is. Make sure that he is comfortable talking to you about his problems, or find an adult that you trust that he can confide in. Teach him to manage his stress levels. During this age, it is very important to discipline your son and set boundaries. Reward your son, but make sure it is tied to him doing the right thing and achieving in school and at home. Also, remember that finding ways to spend time with him will help you to remain a relevant mainstay in his life. Trust that you have prepared him to make the right decisions and if he doesn't, it will be a life lesson to learn accountability.

At eighteen or nineteen years old, your son is legally an adult and will feel invincible. He will expect a certain level of freedom and may begin to limit his communication with you. However, he is communicating with his friends, classmates, and co-workers. At this age, he will begin to make his own choices and routines. If he is in college, when he comes home to visit, he'll want to hang out with friends more than being around you. This is a homecoming for him and time to reunite with childhood and high school friends. If he is working, he may want to hang out with friends from work. He may stay out late. He'll be challenged with choosing between what is acceptable and what is not when it comes to drugs, alcohol, sex and socializing with friends. Emotional concerns like depression and anxiety may hit, but you still need to position yourself as his mother, his parent, and not his friend. Always evaluate yourself and be aware of what you are modeling for him. It is important that you always model adulthood for him.

No matter how difficult it may be to accept, your son will become a man at some point. He won't always be your little boy. Base the freedoms that you give him on where he is developmentally. Even if he seems mature for his age, don't push him too hard too fast. Also, don't hold your son back. Allow him to grow up and become his own man. Give him the freedom to make the right choices. If he doesn't, it's on him to learn the lesson. Teach him to never come out of a bad situation without wisdom, looking at every situation, good or bad, as a learning opportunity. Instill the right values in him and allow him to earn your trust.

Build Trust with Your Son

Trust is built through honesty and practicing integrity. It exists when there is peace, love, joy, patience, kindness, gentleness, self-control, and courage. Children need to experience peace and love in their lives before they can mirror them. The trust your son has for you will be broken if you inflict pain on him mentally, emotionally and physically. When trust is broken, it won't be repaired overnight. That's why it is crucial for you to tell the truth even when it hurts you or your son. Don't lie about certain aspects of your life or his because broken trust will be hard to restore once it is lost.

Be honest with your son. If his father is in prison, tell him the truth about the situation. If his father is not in his life because things didn't work out between the two of you, tell him honestly without bashing his dad in the process. You can be honest without insult. If his father has another woman in his life, don't keep your son away from him because of your jealousy or resentment. Don't tell your son that his father is deceased when he's not or that another man is his father when you know the identity of his real dad. Don't tell your son that his father doesn't want to see him when you know that the father has been trying profusely to be a part of his son's life. Assuming that he is not abusive or a threat to you and your son, he should be in his life.

Do not punish your son if you have moved on with a new man but are still jealous about his father moving on as well. If you have not healed from your son's father's actions, or you're not yet over him or what he did or how he treated you, that is your emotional burden. You didn't deserve to be treated badly, but don't make your son suffer as well. Your desire to see his father hurt for what you experienced is not your son's burden to carry. If you're being disrespectful to your son's father, stop because you're also disrespecting your son and contributing to his resentment toward you. When your son gets older, he will remember how you prevented him from having a healthy relationship with his father and he will treat you accordingly.

I have seen firsthand what happens when mothers manipulate situations. My mother was dishonest with me about who my father really was until I confronted her about it as an adult. I asked her several times to tell me the truth, but she stuck to her original story. After she saw our relationship suffering, she finally told me the truth about my biological father's identity. He had passed away by then. I was very upset with her. I felt like she cheated me out of the opportunity to get to know my real father. She explained why she lied to me, and although I didn't like her answer, I still heard her out. However, our relationship was damaged. Because I was mature and a strong believer in my faith, we were eventually able to move past it. I believe that forgiveness is the first step to restoration. I forgave my mom, we recovered from it, and our relationship is stronger than ever today. Even if you have been dishonest in the past, choose to tell the truth. Go through the process of disappointment that your son will inevitably feel and then work to rebuild the trust in your relationship. It is never too late.

Give Him His Privacy

Something vital you can do for your young son, if it's possible, is to allow him to sleep in his own bed, in his own room. If he has siblings that he shares a room with, you may not be able to make that happen. When he is a baby, for some mothers it can be emotionally and physically draining to put him in his bed, especially in the middle of the night. The turmoil continues when he is a young man, and it seems that letting him sleep in your bed after a long day might be easier. But both of you will benefit it in the long run if he sleeps on his own. It will also allow him to become self-sufficient instead of depending on you. He needs to learn how to do things on his own and you need your own space. Your son might fall asleep in your bed from time to time, but you should put him in his own space early in the night.

That independence will eventually turn into privacy, especially in his teenage years. Respecting your son's privacy means showing him that you trust him to do the right thing. This privacy should also extend to baths. YOUR SON SHOULD NOT BE TAKING BATHS WITH YOU! He needs to learn independence by taking his own baths. As he gets older, he will begin to understand the difference in body parts. Teach him how to clean himself properly, and eventually without your assistance.

In his teenage years, your son's testosterone levels will increase. He will begin to grow hair on his lip and chin, under his arms and in his pubic area. As his hormones rise, so will his aggression, temperament and emotions. You will notice changes in his voice. His body and his thought processes will change also. He may have a growth spurt. His eating habits will change and he will be hungry all the time. Emotionally, he may become defiant and defensive. With all these changes taking place, not having his privacy will effect his temperament.

Some moms think that there is no such thing as privacy in their home. As a result, they insert themselves into every aspect of their sons' lives. Even though it is understood that it is your house, please don't be that mother. If you suspect that your son is doing something irresponsible, have a conversation with him and let him know that he can trust and talk to you. He may still try to hold onto his secret. In that case, send someone else he trusts to speak with him, preferably another man who can relate to what he is going through. At least wait until he leaves for school or to meet up with friends and check things out for yourself. Some would call it being nosy. I would call it saving my son's life. If you have suspicions or a hunch about something, follow your gut. Get ahead of the situation or circumstance.

Give him privacy when he's on the phone. Most young people today have smart phones, so they do a lot of video chatting. He might be on the phone with his girlfriend or male friends often. If you hear something that doesn't sound right, don't force your two cents on him. You were supposed to be giving him privacy, remember? If you suspect something is wrong, listen in on the conversation, but don't be quick to respond. Be sure that what you suspect is really happening before you approach your son.

Showing your son that you respect his privacy is essential to your relationship with him maturing and not going backwards. Respecting privacy and giving him a pass to do whatever he wants are totally different. Until he gets his own place and pays his own bills, he shouldn't be allowed to just do what he wants to do in your house. Rules should be established. If he's making good grades, being respectful to you and others and doing what is asked of him, continue to give him freedom. Check in on him sparingly to ensure that his character matches up with his good grades.

Show Respect

A public setting is not the time to have a discipline 101 class with your son. I have witnessed moms disrespect their sons in public places with anger and frustration instead of love and kindness. You can't put out fire with fire. If he makes a mistake, don't lose your cool. Just correct him with love. He is still learning and developing. If he loses his cool, teach him how to calm himself down.

Your response will determine your son's response. Responding to conflict with patience and empathy will set an example for him. This takes practice and repetition, but you can do it. When faced with an issue, your response is up to you no matter what the issue is. If somebody cuts you off while you are driving, don't stress yourself out cursing and yelling at them. More than likely, the person's window will be up, so they won't hear your expletives anyway. If your son is in the car, he will internalize your reaction and either respond the same way or start putting up a wall against you based on your actions. Your children will never forget an incident where you lost your cool. It stays in their minds because it's traumatizing.

There are calm solutions that won't stress out you or your child. Have you ever been embarrassed in public by someone yelling at you? Just know the other person you yell at feels the same way you felt. Instead of being rude, explain or show the proper way. Make it a teachable moment.

How you discipline your son matters. Do it with care and try your best to teach him something valuable in the process. Use your words wisely because they have power. This means that what you say has value. Speak positive words over your son. Don't punish him just for the sake of it. Humiliating him will only further intensify and magnify the situation between you and him and whoever is watching. Staying calm allows you to have better control.

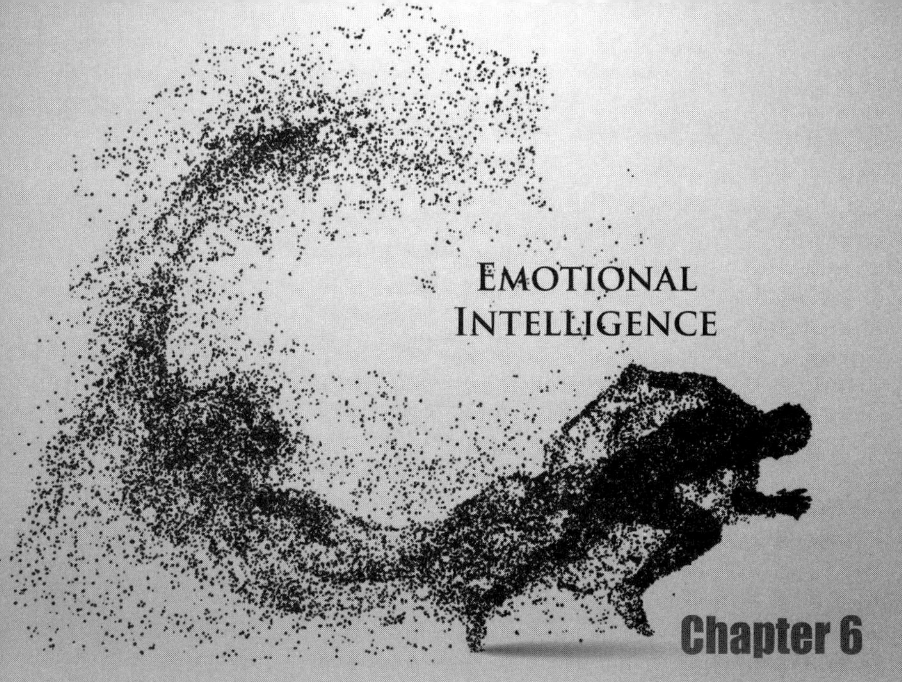

Your emotions and your mindset will determine how you experience life, affect the choices you make and the way you respond to people. It will also play a role in how you deal with yourself. There are five mindsets that you must keep in mind while working to develop emotional intelligence. They are self-awareness, self-regulation, motivation, empathy and social skills. Developing yourself in each of these areas will help you build your emotional intelligence. It's your assignment to manage your emotions as well as your son's.

If you discipline your son by manipulation, anger, or fear tactics, you are not managing emotions. Your emotions are out of control and you are attempting to control him. Anyone who tries to control another person hasn't mastered controlling themselves. Out-of-control emotions are a sign of immaturity. According to Creflo Dollar, "The weakest man (person) on the planet is a man (someone) who cannot control their own emotions." Out-of-control emotions lead to deeper issues like depression, anger, anxiety, and fear.

In the area of developing emotional intelligence, it is imperative that you work on yourself before you can help your son. It is like when you take a flight on an airplane. Before takeoff on any commercial flight, no matter what airline, without fail, the flight attendant instructs on properly using the air mask system. You are instructed, "Should the cabin lose pressure, oxygen masks will drop from the overhead area. Please place the mask over your own mouth and nose before assisting others." We often feel as mothers that we have to help our children first. Yes, helping our children is very important. However, in some cases, like with the oxygen mask, if we don't put the mask on ourselves first, we may run out of air before we are able to help our child then we both suffer.

In the case of emotional intelligence, if we try to help our sons improve their emotional intelligence and we haven't worked on ours, it is a disaster waiting to happen. If you don't have the tools to control yourself while attempting to assist him, you will run into the pitfall of your own out-of-control emotions. Yelling, unjust punishment, saying, "Do as I say and not as I do," and unnecessary overreactions can damage the communication and progress. This could lead to you coming off as judgmental, uncaring, self-righteous and cruel. However, once you have a better understanding of how to control your emotions and have done the work and have seen progress within yourself, you can then help your son manage his emotions with less of a chance of losing your cool.

I have heard people say, "I can't help how I react, it is just how I am," or, "My family members have bad tempers. It is who we are." Despite this long-standing belief held by so many people, the truth is that emotional reactions to people and circumstances are not uncontrollable, they are a choice. When I was younger and "hot-headed," I experienced negative emotions from the actions of other people and outside circumstances. But at the time, I didn't know I was making the choice to be angry, frustrated, sad, or numb. I thought that I had no control over my temper. I often found myself in out-of-control altercations at school. I didn't start fights. I didn't even like to fight, but if someone stepped to me in the wrong way, I quickly retaliated. If someone made disrespectful comments to me or my sisters, my response was overly aggressive and I didn't see anything wrong with it because I felt like I was defending myself and my sisters. I was known as being nice, but people around me knew that if I felt threatened or pushed in a corner that my response would be to come out swinging. I am grateful that my lack of emotional intelligence didn't land me in jail or dead. None of us are exempt from experiencing days when our emotions are heightened, but maintaining your composure and managing how you respond will teach your son how to do the same.

You have a choice to control or not control your emotions. It's up to you to activate your authority over your emotions and gain control. Some of the most effective methods are deliberate prayer/meditation, practicing affirmations, forgiving those who have wronged you, and monitoring and correcting your reactions in undesirable situations. To achieve a higher level of emotional intelligence, you must be willing to be honest with yourself and to discipline your tongue. This will require that you face the disappointments and the pains of your past. It will require that you monitor your reactions to the words and actions of the people around you. There is no overnight remedy for gaining emotional intelligence. But with the right amount of work and self-awareness, you can grow and improve the dysfunction within yourself and your son.

Pitfalls of Poor Emotional Intelligence

Unchecked, some emotions can lead to irreversible life consequences. I knew a young man who became provoked when his teacher wanted to kick him out of class. He was doing his work, but his teacher accused him of talking to another student. He knew he didn't do anything wrong, so he was very passionate with his response. Already in his emotions because of a situation at home, after the teacher yelled at him, the young man got up, threw his books on his desk, and slammed the door behind him. Because of the impact of the door against the frame, the glass in the classroom door broke. Ultimately, no one at the school was concerned that the teacher provoked the young man and falsely accused him of misconduct. Instead, they only focused on his reaction and the broken glass in the door. Because of his response and the teacher saying she feared for her life during the incident, the young man faced expulsion from school. No one questioned the actions of the teacher and chose instead to focus only on the young man's response. Could this happen to your son? Yes, it could. When provoked, would his reaction be questioned and not the actions of the one provoking? There is a good chance.

A video of a young man from the University of Oklahoma went viral a few years ago. In it, a young lady called the young man a derogatory name, used a racial slur and smacked him in the face. Visibly provoked, the young man responded by punching the young lady in her face. While he shouldn't have responded by hitting her back, the young lady was in the wrong for physically assaulting the young man first. Because he was a star athlete in college and an NFL prospect, the media's narrative focused in on the young man's response rather than the young lady's racist comments and physical assault which provoked him in the first place. Men are held to a higher standard, therefore they must learn to control their emotions in all situations.

Even when your son responds in an acceptable way, especially as an African American or Hispanic male, he will be judged. His direct or matter-of-fact answer may often be mistaken for aggression based on someone else's perception of him. Somebody may say something to your son, whether good or bad, but it is his response that matters.

Teach Your Son to be Aware of his Emotions

The psychological, emotional, and spiritual well-being of any child is a parent's responsibility. Developing emotional intelligence is a lifelong journey, and it should be taught and practiced. The benefits of improved emotional intelligence are that your son will feel pride and respect for self. Overall emotional well-being increases both their physical and mental health. Therefore, your son is happier and will have improved self-esteem and confidence.

As a mom, it is your responsibility to prepare him to handle his emotions in every situation whether big or small, good or bad, his fault or someone else's fault. Staying calm is helpful in most every situation. When your son gets upset or heated about a situation at home, don't get angry or frustrated. Use de-escalation techniques, including breathing and allowing him to go into his safe space. Look at it as a teachable opportunity. Teach him to be aware of his tone when speaking to people, especially if he has a passionate nature and is around individuals who may misinterpret his strong personality.

Unfortunately, Black and Brown males are often viewed by many as scary, aggressive, out of control and unable to cope. If your son has had any negative interactions with teachers or administrators, chances are he will be labeled and judged more harshly. That's why he must be taught to respond more effectively to conflict. Prepare him to deal with friends or students at school or in his neighborhood. Boys can be unpredictable; some are outright bullies while others enjoy roughhousing and jabbing each other both verbally and physically. Sometimes the jabs can be harsh and have the potential to get out of control. How your son reacts can make the difference in whether he comes home safely from school or gets suspended, locked up or killed.

Teaching Your Son to Stay Calm in Every Situation

1. Have him to practice breathing techniques
2. Teach him to meditate and/or pray expecting positive outcomes
3. Teach him healthier ways to respond
4. Have him talk to someone about his emotions
5. Teach him to not take every jab personally. Help him to understand that hurt people tend to hurt people due to their trauma. Most of the time it has nothing to do with him personally
6. Explain to him that his actions may be judged harder by those who are in authority because people will view what he does through their perception of him.

5 Mindsets of The Emotional Intelligent

1. **Self-Aware.** Someone who is self-aware makes a deliberate effort to monitor their own emotional state. This person takes a look at their strengths and weaknesses then makes appropriate adjustments.

2. **Self-Regulation.** A self-regulator controls their emotional impulses, including anger, aggression, rage, and jealousy. They think before they respond to adversity. They give themselves time to be thoughtful, adaptable and dependable.

3. **Motivation.** Someone who is self-motivated doesn't need a pep talk from others to perform a task. For them, motivation comes from within. They find different reasons and different ways to motivate themselves to continue to push forward.

4. **Empathy.** Someone who is empathetic understands that people have issues from their past and/or their life circumstances. They don't take other people's actions personally. It doesn't mean they let people run over them. It just means that sometimes, instead of reacting immediately, they wisely step back and objectively look at why a person does or says something instead of rushing to judgment and retaliating.

5. **Social Skills.** The socially skilled understand that everybody is different and can embrace other people's differences. They also understand that individuals must be managed based on their temperament and personality. Socially skilled individuals do well delivering bad news as well as celebrating good news. Either way, everyone around them feels encouraged. They are also comfortable resolving conflict and managing change.

Choose Your Emotions

There is a large range of emotions to choose from, therefore it is important to be aware of and choose emotions that you can recover from. Self-respect is evident through control of your actions and words as governed by your emotional control. Therefore, how you react in drastic situations is a direct reflection of how you view yourself. So, the question is, *how do you view yourself?*

In dealing with others, most people either love or hate each other. In dealing with their emotions, some people are either happy or angry. However, there is a range of emotions in between to acquaint yourself with so that your reaction to people and life isn't always black or white but somewhere in between. Understanding the broad range of emotions at work inside you allows you to better identify how you are truly feeling in any given situation. Some common emotions/feelings/emotional experiences to consider are:

Happy	Bored	Surprised
Loving	Confused	Frustrated
Joyful	Empathetic	Calm
Disgusted	Excited	Pain
Shy	Scared	Entranced
Peaceful	Startled	Relieved
Sad	Afraid	Amused
Angry	Interested	Guilty
Bitter	Ashamed	Embarrassed

The more you are aware of optional feelings to identify with at any moment, the more you realize that you can better express yourself, better understand yourself and become better understood. If you choose to just be angry about the actions of others, you are going to be angry. However, consider that maybe their actions actually made you feel frustrated, or uncovered an old pain, or maybe even made you feel afraid of what the consequences may be. When you take a closer look and express the true emotionyou can have a conversation that could lead to healing instead of an argument.

A Man's Thinking vs. a Woman's Thinking

When it comes to pursuing and choosing a significant other, it is important to be aware that there is a big difference in the way a man thinks versus the way a woman thinks. Men generally choose to approach a woman based off of visual stimulation, while most women are typically a little more concerned about the man's ability to provide financial, emotional, and physical security.

When initially meeting a woman, a man loves what is visually stimulating. Men are visual creatures. A man can see a woman walk across the room and tell himself that he wants to get to know her, date her and possibly be with her for life without even knowing her name yet. Often when a man falls for a woman, he falls in love with her beauty. He falls in love with her eyes, her hair and her curves. In the beginning, he doesn't think about anything else beyond her physical attributes. It doesn't matter if the woman is a waitress, social worker, cook, teacher or businesswoman. If he is visually stimulated, he can see a future with her including vacations, marriage and kids. The woman could be crazy or have serious emotional baggage. She could be in debt up to her eyeballs and have bad credit. She could even be on *America's Most Wanted* for all he knows. However, most men consider none of this when they meet a woman that they're interested in and want to get to know.

Women are different when they meet a man and find him attractive. Within a short period of time, a woman determines whether she wants to be bothered with a man or not. During that time frame, it's similar to a tryout for a sport. A man can make the team or be cut from the team by making one false move. She wants to know if he owns his own house or rents an apartment. She starts asking herself practical questions. Does he still live with his mama? Does he have a job? How much money does he make? How many children does he have? How many baby mamas does he have? Has he been married already? If so, how many times? Is he divorced? If so, what part did he play in the divorce? Does he have all his teeth? What is his credit score? What are his hobbies? What does he like to eat? If she is a vegan or gluten-free, she wants to know if he is too. Where does he hang out? Does he love God? Does he fellowship anywhere? The list goes on.

How the Male Brain Works

Generally, men compartmentalize and focus primarily on what's in front of them. If a man is working on a project, that is where his attention is. If he is watching his favorite basketball team playing either on screen or in person, he is focused on the game and nothing else. If he is on a date with someone he's really interested in, he is focused on the date and the person he is with. A woman can be thinking about 100 things while she is on a date or at a game or while she is working on a project. She is thinking about what she will make for dinner or what she is wearing to work the next day or an assignment she must complete for work. A woman is concerned with what she has on, if her makeup is okay, if her hair is okay. While she is doing all this thinking, she is still present at the date. The man she is with has no idea that all of these things are going through her head. This is because women solve problems using both sides of the brain while a man solves problems using one side of the brain. Men think about what they will wear right before it's time to go somewhere. I explain these differences because I want you moms to know that your sons will not think like you. They will think like them. The key is both men and women understanding each other. Not a full understanding, but something that is manageable.

Men and women are designed differently, and parts of the male and female brain work differently. One of the smallest parts of the male brain has the biggest impact. The amygdala is a small, almond-shaped structure of the brain connected to the end of the hippocampus that helps people process emotions, especially fear and anger. The amygdala tends to be larger in males, which means men have an affinity for more anger, aggression and other intense emotions. The amygdala is also responsible for processing information, as well as learning, motor control, social interactions, and decision making.

Since the amygdala is larger in men, their testosterone levels rise when they are winning and doing well. High testosterone levels mean increased aggression, competitiveness, self-assertion and self-reliance. Healthy competition motivates men. When a young man does well on a test, his testosterone levels are higher. When he wins the girl that he's interested in, his levels go up. Men compete in everything, whether it's getting in line first, being the first one to get to the car to claim a seat or getting to the dinner table first to get the best seat with the best view.

Conversely, a man's testosterone levels decrease whenever he is losing or is depressed. When he loses a game, his levels are low. When he doesn't get the job that he applied for, he can sometimes fall into a depression. When he goes through a divorce, even if he doesn't show emotion, it affects him deeply. If he fails at anything, his emotions along with his testosterone levels are low.

STUDY OF THE MALE BRAIN

1. **Men are more aggressive.** Most men tend to be more aggressive than women in situations having to do with recreational activities, business or projects. Men are also aggressive in pursuing women. They are more likely to ask for a phone number or a date. They are more persistent in their pursuit.

2. **Some Men have Auditory Processing Disorder (APD) or delayed hearing**. People with APD have normal hearing but have a tough time understanding

or processing what is being said to them, especially if a lot of details are involved or the conditions are noisy.

3. **Men are visual.** According to a study led by Emory University psychologists, Stephan Hamann and Kim Wallen, "The emotion control center of the brain, the amygdala, shows significantly higher levels of activation in males viewing sexual visual stimuli than females viewing the same images."

4. **Men don't ask for help unless it's crucial.** Men don't like asking for assistance. It's good that we have GPS now because most men don't like to stop and ask for directions when they are lost. When creating, fixing, or restructuring, some men want to take all the credit for themselves and not share the glory with others. A man will tear up your house trying to fix something because he is always trying to impress his significant other. When she is impressed, he feels accomplished.

5. **Men believe their ability is all they need to succeed.** A man will trust his God-given ability whether it be his athleticism, his musical talents, his intellect, or his business savvy, believing that it's all he needs to accomplish his goals. Once he has determined that his skill is worthwhile, he will confidently move forward against all obstacles or doubt.

You play a role in how your son manages his aggression based on what you did or didn't do when he was a child. If you failed to administer the proper discipline or consequences, then you have work to do. When a young man acts out in an aggressive manner, it's for a reason and that reason needs to be examined. Find out why and get to the bottom of it while he is young. If your son happens to be older and you couldn't do this when he was younger, it's not too late, but it will take some time and effort on your part. It also goes back to him learning how to manage and control his emotions. On the other hand, if he is punished for little to no reason or subjected to trauma repeatedly, it will adversely affect him in his adult years. Be aware that either your uncontrollable anger or your lack of giving consequences in his childhood can lead to your son's uncontrollable anger and tendency toward violent acts.

According to Dr. Jacqueline E. Fahey, author of *The Impact of the Mother-Son Relationship on Expression of Aggression in Young Adulthood*, the more involved a mother is during her son's childhood, the less aggressive he tended to be in young adulthood. The more nurturing the mother, the less likely her son expresses aggression in young adulthood. If a son was subjected to corporal punishment during childhood, he would be more likely to be aggressive in young adulthood. This means you need to be involved with your son early and often. Nurturing your son has a more positive impact than using corporal punishment. However, work to find a balance when nurturing, so that you don't overdo it.

When a male child is born, sometimes he is already stereotyped through toxic masculinity. Fathers, cousins, and uncles start predicting his future, calling him the next great athlete, entertainer or business owner before he speaks his first words. He is compared to his parents' favorite celebrities or actors. When disciplining the young boy as he ages, some parents and relatives unfortunately use phrases which teach toxic masculinity. Examples include:

- Man up!
- Don't show emotion!
- Stop being a punk!
- Stop being soft!
- Stop being a sissy!
- Men don't cry!
- Be tough!
- Don't be weak!

Most of our sons have been hearing these phrases from a very young age. Such strong assertions can cause a young man to be confused. Toxic words define the behavior of young men, causing them to become defensive, defiant and combative. Mothers make damaging comments and put negative labels on their sons without thinking about the consequences and the personality shaping. When mothers negatively inundate their sons, they often watch them mature into the very labels they put on them. From then on, they go about wondering what is wrong with their son. Not realizing that a great deal of the damage came from their words. Our words hold more power than we know. They have the ability to build or tear down.

A mother may not have used negative criticisms toward her son, but he might have gotten them from his father, male cousins, uncles or peers. Consequently, everyone seems surprised when he grows up acting out the labels that have been put on him. I grew up being told to "man up" and not show emotion so much that those words became part of my mantra. I wanted to prove I was a man, so I kept my feelings to myself in most situation. To prove my manhood, I would fight if someone looked at me wrong. The effects of toxic masculinity made me an angry, bitter young man struggling to control my emotions.

I would make outburst, get into arguments, get suspended from school for fighting. No one seemed to be concerned with the source of my issues or how to help me make better choices. I would get punished and everyone moved on until the next incident. Your son could be holding on to some of these same emotions that need to be released. Young men are expected to figure it all out often with very little guidance or positive reinforcement.

We are all busy, but find the time to engage with your sons early. Nurturing is another healthy way to connect to your son through his growth and development as a young man. Do what is right, not what is popular. All kids should be held accountable for their actions, but some punishments are unnecessary and cruel. For example, slapping your son for not taking the trash out is extreme and uncalled for. Corporal punishment is wrong, especially for minor offenses. Not only is it belittling to your son, but more importantly it takes away his right to human dignity. It will also cause your son to be more aggressive at school, in the neighborhood and on the school bus.

The way you treat your son as a child will determine how he treats others when he becomes an adult. If you shake up a can of Sprite and open it, it will explode. Some mothers have witnessed men exploding and losing their tempers, including your sons. Where did this originate? What part did you play in his behavioral issues? It happens when young men hold on to built-up childhood trauma. Failing to understand the way your son thinks or choosing to belittle him or issuing discipline with messages that promote toxic masculinity, will cause him to have out-of-control emotions as an adult. You must get to the root of anger to fix the problem.

The Root of Anger

If a man is angry about anything, he's fearful, frustrated or in pain about something. Fear is a secondary emotion. People experience anger because of being hurt, betrayed, jealous, embarrassed, guilty or ashamed. Instead of asking your son why he is so angry, ask him what he is fearful of, what is hurting him or why he is frustrated. Try and help him identify the primary emotion that is fueling his fear. Dealing with the primary emotions generally helps to solve the real issue at hand.

Pain is pain and hurt is hurt. There's nothing we can do about what has already happened. If you are the culprit, a simple apology and change in your actions for the better will help smooth out a bad situation and allow your son to move forward. However, repeating the same behavior and actions will cause more pain. Unaddressed, that pain will lead to anger.

If his anger causes a physical reaction, teach your son it's not okay to kick or punch walls or throw furniture when he is upset. It is not okay to abuse a woman, even if she is acting irrationally. It is not okay to disrespect adults and others because he is hurting, even when they are wrong. His pain and anger cannot be used as an excuse to hurt others. Society isn't always kind to young men when circumstances arise that provoke them to explode and lose control. Stay ahead of inevitable adversity by giving your son strategies to cope.

Understanding How a Man Processes His Emotions

Some women think men are emotionless. That is far from the truth. Men can tap into softer emotions like love, caring and affection, but life, their environment and loved ones have conditioned them to primarily show their tough side and defer revealing their true emotions and feelings. This means their feelings are suppressed, which explains why so many men, young and old, get quiet and don't say anything in the midst of sensitive situations. In most cases, it's not that a man doesn't care; on the contrary he does, but he contains his true feelings. He may not want to come off as "emotional." Men experience more emotions than most women, but too many are conditioned to never feel safe enough to react authentically.

Once they are reassured it's safe to do so, men will show softer emotions. For him to share the true range of the emotions that he experiences, a man must trust the person he displays them around. Otherwise, he will keep them buried deep. He will instead show how he feels through his actions. If he is happy, he may hug you or may simply smile. If he is feeling anxious, he may pull back from the crowd or want to stay in for the night. If he is feeling sad, he may not say much during the conversation when you try to talk to him.

As a young man, I had a tough time coming out of my shell. I never felt comfortable enough to do so. My mom worked a lot and had many things on her plate at the time, so I couldn't express my feelings to her. I never told her that I had a difficult time sleeping while she worked late. We never talked about it. I never went into a spiel about how worried I was for her most nights. I never told her that I didn't stop worrying about her until the moment she walked through the door. Instead, every night I slept by the front door to make sure I knew the moment she got home safe. Once the door hit my back when she opened it, I would go to my room, where I slept better knowing she was home.

I didn't grow up with my biological father and two of the men my mom chose to allow in our home were abusive. One was physically abusive and the other physically and emotionally abusive. It's tough growing up with poor examples of men. It puts young men at a disadvantage growing into his manhood. Although I didn't express it back then, I felt angst at school, in my neighborhood and when those men were in my house. I had no place to turn for refuge. There was pressure on every end. I felt scared, on edge, unsupported, lonely, misunderstood, and uncomfortable most of my waking hours. A lot of young men feel this way and never express it. Nonetheless, I just suppressed those feelings. I was angry and didn't feel comfortable enough to share those emotions with anyone, not even my mother. Instead, I tried to hide how I felt by participating in sports. It seemed to be working until later in life when I was cut from the Minnesota Vikings NFL team. Then I was forced to deal with my suppressed anger and emotions.

When a man comes off as if nothing phases him: like he's got everything under control, it is a facade. If you see him experiencing turmoil or conflict, understand that just because he doesn't discuss it doesn't mean that it isn't affecting him deeply. So, when something that seems trivial and small causes him to explode, understand that a host of emotions had been brewing within him all along.

Hard and Soft Skills

By now, you understand that anger and rage surface because of a young man's lack of emotional intelligence and bottling up emotions that he has no intention of releasing. When those emotions are not addressed, they turn into hopelessness, depression and anxiety. Eventually, a young man that started out considerate and well-mannered will grow into a man who is rude, uncaring, and emotionless.

If a person is angry and upset every day, it puts a strain on the mind and body, which later turns into sickness. Hypertension leads to all kinds of other health problems like kidney failure, diabetes or heart attack. Overall, men of all races have a much higher death rate than women due to heavy workloads and premature health issues. All this is to say, stress alone can cause serious health issues.

Hard emotions like anger and depression can only be reversed when met with softer actions, including respect, trust, empathy, honesty, communication and calmness. If your son comes in angry, teach him the importance of emotional intelligence and how to properly express himself. If your son feels disappointment, teach him that disappointments are a part of life and show him the importance of recovering from setbacks. If he is struggling with feelings of neglect, show him that you see him and teach him the importance of self-love and appreciation. If he is wrestling with rage, teach him how to meditate and remain calm.

Choosing to embrace happiness, joy and peace is also important for countering anger. Get to the bottom of why your son is angry by responding to his frustration with peace and kindness. Be at ease when speaking with him. When he is angry be firm, but prepared to manage his temperament, while maintaining yours. Help him get to the root of the problem. It's never too late to help your son repair the issues he may have suppressed. Don't be afraid to discuss and work through past hurts with him, even if he is a grown man.

The Hidden Pain in Men

Men appear to be able to handle pain better than women. That is not necessarily true. After studies and much debate through the years, the verdict is still out regarding emotional pain. Women tend to show their feelings more often, but they seem to be more forgiving. If a man cheats on a woman, in some cases she will choose to stay in the relationship for financial stability, needing help with the kids and overall security. Most men couldn't handle a woman cheating on him and would probably leave if he found out about it. A woman may or may not leave the relationship. If the problem is public and in her face, she is more prone to leave. If the issue is private, chances are she handles it privately and may decide to stay.

I used to watch my mother and grandmother take hot pans out of the oven with their bare hands. I couldn't believe they were touching a hot item and not screaming in pain. I have never seen a man take a hot pan out of an oven without mittens or a towel to protect him from being burned. In my experience, women have shown to have a higher pain threshold then men in this way.

The difference in pain is also based on individual experiences and upbringings. When women are in emotional pain, they express those emotions by crying, yelling or being silent. When a woman is upset, the whole atmosphere changes. A man is different. You don't always know if he's suffering from emotional pain or just having a bad day. He sometimes puts on a poker face or laughs and smiles like everything is cool even when he is hurting. This is a defensive mechanism.

You may never know your son is hurt unless he tells you. Some men even get so comfortable concealing pain that they become immune and no longer acknowledge the pain. A man could have been abused or molested as a kid, but he would go about his life like none of it ever took place because the pain is suppressed. Men who are in emotional pain sometimes seem outwardly unavailable and uncaring. This is displayed for example when a woman cries in front of a man, but he doesn't react. He seems to feel no sympathy. When a man reacts this way, he has been through a great deal of pain himself. Maybe he has watched his mother and other family members cry so much that tears don't move him anymore. In fact, in the back of his mind, he may think the tears are fake depending on the circumstance. It is the unaddressed pain and heartache from his own past hurt that causes him to become numb, tearing him down from the inside out. Consequently, these men are unable to give and receive emotional ques in a healthy way.

You do not want this to happen to your son, so the following are four steps to be aware of that you can share with your son as he works to overcome pain that he has experienced in the past:

Four Steps to Overcoming Pain

1. **Acknowledge that you are in pain.** You must first admit that you are in pain. Taking ownership is a solid step to beginning the healing process.

2. **Write down what you're in pain about** to release it from your spirit. You may choose to journal consistently or as the pain hits you.

3. **Speak to someone** you trust. Speaking about your pain is therapeutic and healing. As you heal, you may feel strong enough to use your pain as your own testimony to help others.

4. **Forgive** the person who hurt you, not for them, but for your own healing. You may never forget, but you can forgive. Forgive yourself. Punishing yourself will not help matters. Forgiving yourself frees you to move forward to make better decisions in the future. Forgiving the other person frees you from the bondage of holding a grudge and having misplaced anger toward those around you.

Communicate with Love and Respect

Love and respect go hand in hand when building healthy relationships. When someone says they love you with their words, but are disrespectful with their actions, they contradict themselves. Our sons experience and witness so much disrespect in the world whether in school at the park, in their neighborhood, on social media, and on TV. It is important that we set the standard by having a solid foundation of love and respect at home.

There are obviously a lot of things that you will need to teach your son as he develops into a man. However, the most important yet underrated principle that you can instill in him is the ability to love himself and others. For your son, showing himself love and loving others starts with a deeper understanding of what love is and its importance. Love is patient, kind, gentle and consistent. Teach your son to show love by being honest and polite, taking care of other's property, controlling his temper, and admitting when he's wrong.

Also, teach him to demonstrate love through acceptance and respect. Respect is a deep admiration for someone, displayed by regarding one's feelings, rights, traditions and wishes. Essentially, it's the way you treat someone. Respect is humble, peaceful, polite, and considerate. Respect and love go together.

Respect for men and women is different because we think differently. If your son feels disrespected during a conversation, whatever you say to him will not be received. He will also feel unloved. Your goal when communicating with him is mutual respect. To make sure he receives the information, it is important to approach him in love.

Your son may feel like you blatantly disrespect him often and, in some cases, you may feel the same way about him. His lack of respect doesn't necessarily mean lack of love for you. Your son loves you but, he would show it more if he felt like you respected him. If you find yourself going back and forth with your son, understand that both of you are dealing with properly showing love and respect for one another. Let him know that you are trying. If it applies, help him to understand that as a kid you didn't get the proper guidance and therefore didn't know how to teach him. Be honest with him. When you fall short, don't make excuses. Apologize and agree to start fresh. Ask your son what he needs from you and listen to his response. Tell him what you need from him. Be forgiving of each other when you fail and work together to get back on track. Tell him that just like him, you are learning how to be more respectful.

Show love and respect for your son through verbal and nonverbal communication. Verbally tell your son that you hear him, appreciate what he is saying and understand from his viewpoint. Non-verbally, show him that you hear him by active listening, turning, and looking at him when he is speaking. Nod in response. When speaking with your son, don't just use the words respect and disrespect to describe his actions. Instead, use the words love, appreciate, disappointed, misunderstood or concerned.

Teach your son that some people are vindictive and manipulative. Everyone will not have his best interest in mind. Let him know the importance of guarding his heart. He has to carefully choose who he allows in his circle. However, when he knows that the person is genuine, not perfect, he can safely let down his guard. Let your son know that it is important to love himself and to display it in the way he interacts with the people in his life. Encourage him to forgive himself and to forgive others. Teach him to have healthy conversations that allow him to respect himself and the people he cares about.

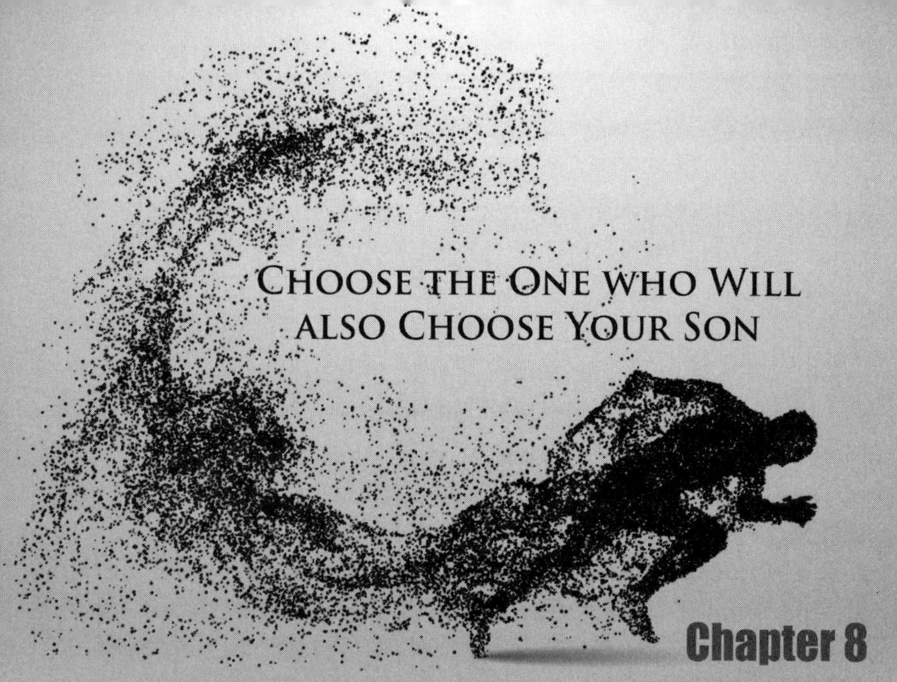

Weighing Your Options

If you are already married, I pray that you are in a good, healthy relationship. Choosing your soul mate is tough in today's world. People hide behind their social media pages, pretending to be someone they're not. They lie about their credentials, relationship status and family. You sometimes meet someone's representative instead of the real person. Nonetheless, because you have a son, it is imperative that you properly discern the kind of person that you allow into your private life. Not only do you need to concern yourself with how a significant other would treat you, but you would also need to concern yourself with how they would treat your son.

You may not know exactly what you want, but you need to have an idea of how you want life with a significant other to look. It's important to consider how they will interact with you. Are they considerate, attentive, patient, or are they self-centered, distracted and distant? Pay attention if they yell or are disrespectful with their words. Do they stay out all night? Is your potential mate someone who doesn't want to work? Do they complain constantly about the job that they currently have? Do they prioritize your needs? That's a good start but you can't stop there because you have a son. It is so important that you observe how your significant other interacts with your child and how he reacts to your son in general. Does he seem happy to see him, or is he annoyed by your son's presence? Does he attempt to talk to him, or does he act like he isn't in the room? If the person doesn't seem to show an interest in your son in the beginning of the relationship, don't assume that things will get better. More than likely things will get progressively worse. When someone shows you who they are, believe what you see.

To get a better sense of who your potential significant other is, watch their interactions with the people in their life. How do they interact with their mother and/or their children? What you are looking for is the ease of conversation, the considerate checking up and what they say about them in general conversations. They can't be a good mate for you if they disrespect their own mother and they can't be a good role model to your son if they aren't good role models to their own children.

You need a reliable mate. Your son needs a good role model. Don't ignore the signs. If the man you're with starts off lying about small things, you will not be able to trust him with big things. I tell women all the time to be honest with themselves, they can't change a man's actions. He must want to change for himself.

In order to attract the right kind of mate that fits you and your family dynamics, you must know exactly who you are. You must know your wants, needs and desires. You cannot compromise on your deal-breakers. It is not that you need a perfect mate, but you do want someone whose pros enhance your life and whose cons are tolerable. If you are with someone who has done things to compromise your trust in the relationship, but who is actively trying to get themselves together, they may deserve a second chance to get it right. Still, make clear your limits and expectations and stick by them.

If you are a believer and the man that you're with is not seeking God's heart and not a believer, RUN! If he is a believer, there is a chance that he will try to get it right. Don't get fooled by men who say they are believers with their mouth, but their actions show different. If you and your mate are not equally yoked, it will not work. You should know this before moving forward. It doesn't matter how much money he has. It doesn't matter about his physique or facial features, waves, curls or whatever you like. If he doesn't believe in God, it will be difficult to find common ground when growing your relationship and in raising your son. If he is seeking God, be friends with him and give the relationship some time. Remember that no one is perfect but find out if he wants to improve himself or if he just uses God's words to justify his actions.

When it comes to finances, it is important to consider who will be the bread winner in your relationship. If your potential mate does not work or pay his own bills, what makes you think he's going to assist you with yours? If he can't take care of his own basic needs, how will he take care of yours and your son's? If it is agreed upon that you are going to be the primary provider and he is going to take care of the children and the home, that is a different situation. However, if you expect him to take care of the home while you work or if you expect him to work while you take care of the home, you must make that agreement up front. So many women come home to men sitting on their couch, playing video games, or watching TV and not contributing anything to the household. If this is you, you must ask yourself, did I make my expectations clear in the beginning? If you didn't, now is a good time to have the hard discussions. As a result of the discussion, you can then decide how you want to move forward. If he is willing to be a homemaker, it may work for your family, but if he isn't he may have to go. Just don't compromise your vision for a stable family life to have a man in your house.

Another way to get to know a new love interest is to speak to him about his past relationships. Do some research. If you are unsure about how he thinks, don't hesitate to ask questions. If he has had five failed relationships in the past two years, inquire about the details. Just be sure to be conversational and not interrogating. Find out why each of the relationships ended. What went wrong? Be aware if every bad relationship that he was in was someone else's fault. I'm not saying that he needs to take full responsibility for every failed relationship, but he does have to own up to his part. Usually there are mistakes made by both parties.

If you notice that you two haven't been on a date, ask him what kind of dates he and his exes went on. If he says he doesn't believe in dating, then if you are expecting him to take you on a date, you are wasting your time. If he doesn't mind dating, ask him what some of the places are that he'd like you two to go for future dates.

There are so many different sides to a person, but the only way to find out about them is to have the courage to ask. You don't have to make a potential mate feel like he is being interviewed, just find opportune moments to ask pertinent questions within the flow of conversation. If your potential mate doesn't want to answer your questions, then he is most likely hiding his true self from you. Don't wait around to see what he reveals years later because more than likely the things that he is hiding are the things that will bring stress and turmoil to you and your son's life. Don't ignore any information you receive while doing your research because ignoring the signs only prolongs the inevitable. When you make a decision to potentially share you and your son's life with someone, guessing and hoping will not be enough. Careful thought, attention to detail and having realistic expectations will help you to make a sounder decision.

Blending Families

The older you get, the more likely your union with a significant other will result in a blended family. Blending families can be tough, especially if each parent doesn't discuss and explain up front the expectations and the current situation with the other parent. I had my first child at the age of twenty-seven and I was a single father. When my wife and I were dating, my son was only five years old. She didn't have children then. My wife didn't immediately meet my son when we were dating, because I didn't know where the relationship was going. However, I made it clear from the beginning of our relationship how important my son was to me. When we decided to get serious and started talking about what a long-term relationship would look like, I had a conversation with her about the significance of my son on my life decisions. I made it clear that my son and I came as a package deal. I wanted her to understand that she could not have a serious relationship with me if she couldn't see him integrated into our day-to-day lives. I also let her know that my son's mother didn't communicate well with me or try to get along peacefully for the sake of our son. Because I was up front with my wife about my son's mother's personality, she understood who she was and how to deal with her and there was never any friction between the two of them.

At the time, we lived in a city neither of us wanted to make our permanent residence, but my son was there. She understood that I would not be interested in moving at least until he graduated from high school. I had already gone through the pain of not having a father while growing up, so I didn't want my son to experience that. He needed a father and I wasn't going to abandon him even though I had a toxic relationship with his mother. It was a sacrifice, but I wasn't willing to compromise. When my wife finally met my son, they hit it off well. I was surprised that they got along so quickly. She was genuine with him, and they have built a strong relationship that has grown over the years. Although she didn't care for the city, she chose me and my son. If you have children already, make sure that the man you date understands that he cannot have you without your kids. If this is a problem for him, make sure that he knows this is a problem for you.

Occasionally, mothers too quickly introduce random guys to their sons. I always made it clear that my son played a vital role in my life, but I was never in a rush to introduce him to the women I dated. I wanted to make sure that my son didn't grow attached to someone who I knew would only be in our lives for a short period of time.

When you casually date someone with no intention of commitment, sometimes feelings get involved. An unplanned pregnancy could take place or other circumstances may find you two bound to one another. When you don't share with him in the beginning who you are and what is important to you, everything is left up to interpretation. In his mind, he may not know just how important a factor your son is to you. Don't leave the significance of your relationship with your son unaddressed. If your feelings get wrapped up in someone and you're not sure if he will accept your kids, it becomes stressful and awkward. From the beginning try to find out his view as best as you can and make your decisions about continuing the relationship accordingly.

Make sure it is clear from the start that if a significant other is to be in your life that your son will need to have significance in his life too. If the relationship is meaningful, there comes a time when the introduction needs to be made, but not too quickly. You must see where the relationship goes first. When you are certain that you've made a long-term match, make sure that you set up a proper time for your potential mate to meet your son. Please don't let it be that your son comes in from school and the guy has already moved in and is lounging on your sofa with his feet kicked up on the coffee table, with the remote in hand. It would be better received by both parties if everyone knows in advance so they will be expecting the meeting.

A man who doesn't accept your children shouldn't even be in the picture. There are multiple reasons why. If your son knows he isn't accepted, he will feel rejected. Also, chances are a man who doesn't accept your son is more likely to be dismissive, uncaring or abusive. There are so many stories of men who rape, beat and neglect children of the women they are involved with. It is not worth the stress, confusion or negative energy to your son to allow someone into your environment who is interested in you, but indifferent towards your son.

If you are a single mother and your potential mate is a single father, before committing, a few visits should take place at both your place and his. This will allow your son to be comfortable in both settings. Please don't move too fast by moving in together. By all means, don't get married first before your families meet each other. Families should be blended slowly and strategically. It helps you and all involved, including exes, to prepare for the transition. All the children need to be introduced and should have the opportunity to spend time together beforehand, so that they can get comfortable with the idea of new people joining their family. It will give you the opportunity to see how they get along and to come up with bonding opportunities, like going out for a meal, playing a game at home, playing kickball, taking a group walk in the park or taking a group trip.

A slow transition will allow you to prepare yourself for the additional people that may come with the new union, including the potential of judgmental parents, drama-filled baby mamas, and other meddling or uncouth relatives. You may never have to deal with these kinds of people, but you don't want to be blindsided if you do.

Building a Relationship Between Your Man and Your Son

As you build your relationship with your new significant other, be sure to foster a growing relationship between your man and your son. Schedule a meeting in a neutral setting in public. Pay attention to how he interacts and responds to your son. Be patient with the process. Don't try and force a connection. Let it happen organically. Relationships take time and you and your significant other must be willing to put in the time to develop this new connection.

Your new man must respectfully integrate himself into your lives. Before he is put into the position to discipline your son, you and he should have had a conversion discussing discipline styles. If you both agree on a discipline style, great. If not, you must come to some sort of an understanding or there will be major problems down the line. Until an agreement has been made, he should not be directly involved in a discipline situation that you are handling. But discussing it afterwards will help you two get a better understanding of the other's point of view.

To help nurture their relationship, there should be time set aside for him to spend one-on-one time with your son. It would be ideal if he chose to do this on his own, but if he doesn't, just make the suggestion and set it up if need be. His response to this request will tell you everything you need to know. Although it is important that you two continue to date, there should definitely be times when you, your significant other, your children and his children, if he has any, get together. The main thing is that you both remain positive and patient, and not enter the relationship immediately changing things. If immediate changes need to be made, make sure it's in the best interest of your son.

A Toxic Man in Your Home

Some mothers fall in love and settle down with a man only to find that he is toxic to their environment. Men who have out-of-control emotions are toxic. They don't know themselves and don't know how to operate as part of a healthy relationship. Toxic men don't care about their children or yours. They are insecure and can't control their own emotions and will therefore attempt to control you and your son. Some toxic men don't want to work or provide for you and your son. Instead, they will live off you, while bringing negative energy into your home, as long as you will allow him to do so.

A toxic man may physically, emotionally, mentally, psychologically, or even sexually abuse you and potentially your son. He doesn't talk or try to reason. Instead, he yells, is easily agitated and dictates the actions of those around him. You may barely know this man, but a toxic man will show signs early on, so pay attention.

If a man is unwilling to apologize or evaluate himself or step back and make changes when he has made mistakes, leave him. A man stuck in his ways is the worst kind of man to be around. If he abuses drugs or alcohol, this will affect you and your children. A toxic man will need money for his habits, so it will drain his resources and yours. A sober mind is needed to make sound decisions, so if he is always intoxicated, how can he properly lead your household? Pay attention to the signs and be honest with yourself. Be prayerful and have faith. All you need to know will be revealed.

My mom dated a man when my sisters and I were young. I saw the two of them together, but to me he was just a man that my mother was dating. A short period of time later, he moved in with us. It was never conveyed to me that they had decided that he would move in. It was never conveyed to me that he would become a part of my everyday life. He was just there. There were no visits prior to him moving in that I recall and there was no time to adjust. He and my mother chose to live together, but never married. He treated me badly from day one, always fussing at me for trivial things and being physically and verbally abusive, especially when my mom wasn't around. She eventually broke up with him, but the damage to me and my sisters had already been done. That guy inflicted emotional and physical damage on us that affected us well into our adult lives.

After a few short years, my mom started dating a new guy. During the short time that they dated, he kept his interaction with me to a minimum. When or if he chose to speak, it felt as if it was out of obligation and not genuine interest. Like the last situation, he moved in with us, too. As far as I was concerned, he was a stranger in our house. Then suddenly he and my mom were married. I don't recall going to the wedding or there being a ceremony. There was no discussion or even a clue to alert me that they would be married, but somehow, we had become a dysfunctional, disengaged family. He was close to my sisters, but not me. It created the impression that it was them and, oh, by the way, I was there too. For me, it never felt like an "us."

He never went to my football games in high school. After graduation, I attended and played football at Western Kentucky University. I garnered a lot of attention because I was one of the few freshmen who received playing time. I was a 4-year starter in college. For the first time, he decided to show interest in me and my accomplishments as a football player. He came to one of my games. We won and after the game he and my mother came on the field to congratulate me. A reporter stopped him for questions. The man who I had no connection with, who abused me mentally and physically, who I never even had a real conversation with had the nerve to tell a reporter that I was his son. He and my mom had been together for ten years and never had he claimed or affirmed me as his son until that moment. He waited until I was a college athlete to recognize me as his son. For me, it was too little too late.

Does your man really accept your son or does he do just enough to stay off your radar? Does he work to build a meaningful relationship of respect and trust with your son or does he just exist around him? Mothers, when it comes to incorporating a love interest into your family, he needs to know that your son is not just another person in the house, but that he is a meaningful part of your life. If he has an issue with that, walk away. The mistreatment, abuse or neglect that children experience in blended families produces men who later have issues with trust, love, affection and forgiveness. You are not married to your son, but he still has feelings and emotions. He is a human being. When in a committed relationship, a real man takes care of another man's child. Commit to only settling down with a potential mate who will be willing to treat your son like his own child.

What to Do if Your Son Puts Up a Wall

If your husband or boyfriend is really trying, but your son is rebelling against him, you must step in and have a conversation with your son right away. If you are divorced or separated from your son's biological father, he may decide to reject any new man in your life. Your son needs to know that your man will never replace his father, but you intend to move forward with him in your life. Hear me, your son cannot dictate what you do with your life or who you decide to date. However, you should be sensitive to his feelings. This new relationship will take time and effort. Just like the man must try, your son must give him an opportunity as well.

Break down this barrier between your man and your son by finding common ground between the two. Does your son like football, basketball, baseball, swimming, video or board games? Your new husband may not know how to do any of these activities, but if your son likes one of them, then your man could develop a new interest to connect to your son. He can also introduce him to some of his interests. Once common ground has been found, it becomes easier for your son to connect on subjects and hobbies that your new love enjoys. This will teach your son new activities as well, which will be good for him.

Your man can show up to your son's games or events for support. He doesn't have to say anything or make a big show about being there. Your son's walls will start coming down when he spots him in the stands supporting his efforts and cheering him on, with or without you. You know your son better than anybody, so your input will go a long way. Bring it to your son's attention that the new person in your lives is trying to get to know him. Share with him the importance of them bonding. Let him know although your family is expanding, he is still equally important to you.

The New Baby

One of the biggest issues that can arise with blended families is when it is announced that a new baby is on the way. Even if your son is included in the anticipation of the birth, he may likely feel left out and isolated at times. A newborn is usually adored by mom, dad and relatives from both sides of the family. If your son is used to being the only child in your life, or he feels like there are already too many siblings in the family, he may rebel when he finds out about the new addition to your family. Be proactive. Your son should be one of the first people to know about your pregnancy. Also, spending one-on-one time with your son is crucial. It's important to reserve love and affection for your son so that he doesn't grow to resent you, your husband or the baby.

When it was just you and your children, they may have become accustomed to being the center of your attention. They may become uneasy knowing that not only did they have to start sharing you with your new husband, who is not their biological father, but they will now also have to accept a new sibling on the way. This could cause further division in a family where there is already unresolved dysfunction. However, if handled properly, this could turn out to be a good situation.

Make sure your son establishes a relationship with his little brother or sister before the baby comes into the world. Once it arrives, a new baby needs attention around the clock, and this will be challenging for your son. With all the affection and attention the new baby is receiving your son may feel insignificant. While you are still carrying, let him talk to your belly, get acquainted with his new sibling or even feel the baby kick. When the child is born, let your son bond with his new sibling by immediately holding the baby, depending on his age. Allow him to assist in small ways in caring for the child. Even if it's only for five minutes, allow him to do something for his new baby brother or sister.

I have three children who watch how I treat each of their siblings. My son was eight or nine years old when his younger sister was born. He stayed the night with my wife and I at the hospital, so he was there when she was born. Whenever I kissed his sister, I hugged and kissed him also. I worked hard to make him feel included. My wife also tried to make him feel a part of the excitement by asking him about potential baby names and asking him what he wanted the baby to call him once she could talk. Even still, he eventually felt left out at times. Although he and his stepmother got along well, he missed the idea of having both of his parents together. After all, the new baby had both her parents. All I could do was reassure him with my words and actions that he still meant the world to me and his stepmother.

You also should spend one-on-one time with just you and him whenever possible, even if it is for small moments of time. Leave your baby at home with your husband and take him out for ice cream or to pick up dinner. This allows you and your son to have bonding time and lets him know that he still matters. Your husband should also spend one-on-one time with your son without you being present. I did this often with my own son after my daughters were born because the one-on-one time is so important. Taking him to the movies was one of our many activities together. I believe this is one of the reasons why my children are extremely tight today. I continue to spend one-on-one time with him and each of my two daughters as well. And the three of them spend sibling time together.

Your son is not your significant other's biological child, but when he married you, your son should have become his son as well. Make sure your husband understands his role in your blended family. Yes, you two may have a new baby together, but you had a child before the new one arrived and his presence should be appreciated, supported and respected. Your husband should therefore spend time with him and work to forge a relationship with all the children in your blended family.

Talk to Your Son About Sex

According to Planned Parenthood, 50% of all teenagers feel uncomfortable speaking with their parents about sex, while 19% of parents felt the same way about speaking to their children. This means many children don't speak with their parents about questions they have about sex. At the same time, a number of their parents are also avoiding the conversation all together. When parents choose to avoid such an important yet uncomfortable topic, their children are forced to figure it out on their own through friends and social media. When parents do talk about sex in a way that is preachy and lacking understanding, using phrases like, "don't go out and get a disease," and "you'd better not get her pregnant," your son can feel that you are overbearing, nosy and controlling. Nonetheless, it is important to push past the communication barriers, so your son feels comfortable enough to speak with you about sex.

Sex is a part of our everyday life and it needs to be discussed. It's okay to talk with your son about sex by the age of eleven or twelve or depending on his environment, maybe sooner. This is important because his body is changing and he has many questions. He and his friends may have already had conversations about sex, not necessarily safe sex. If he doesn't want to be left out, he will chime in, pretending that he is aware of the topic being discussed. He may not have decided about crossing the line yet, but he could be getting close. This is a good time to discuss sex in more detail.

You may think there is no way your son is thinking about having sex. Don't be fooled. Think about yourself at his age or remember the young men who attempted or successfully persuaded you. Take the pressure you dealt with growing up and multiply it. This is the pressure your son feels now. Young people are given incorrect and sometimes harmful advice about sex through social media, lyrics in songs or raps, inappropriate friends and disrespectful relatives. If your son's closest friends talk confidently to him about sex, your son is bound to follow their advice. It is important for you to step in and get to him first, teaching him with love, care and honesty.

If he tells you that he likes a certain young lady, it is a good time to explain relationships, emotions, the ups and downs of relationships and sexual activity. Ask him to tell you some qualities that he is looking for in a young lady. Acknowledge and address every quality he mentions, then give him a few gentle suggestions, including how to approach her, a good way and time to follow up and how not to be too persistent. This is another way to connect with him. If he seems a little uncomfortable with the conversation, tell him it's okay and that you understand, but don't be pushy. Still, continue to guide him. Try not to pour too much on him up front. Ask a few questions and let him speak freely, then you can chime in as needed.

According to the *Child Development Institute* article, "Discussing Sex with Your Teenage Son," "Sexism and objectification of women is unfortunately a normal part of society, and something that teenagers absorb from the media. Teenage boys-and even young adults-often view sexual conquest as a status symbol." It also stated that sex with young ladies is glorified in school hallways and locker rooms. Women are disrespected in so many ways, so it is important that you teach the foundation and principles about respecting women and not treating them like objects who have no feelings, no matter how they see themselves.

Start from where he is, whether your son is five or fifteen years old. Of course, you would have a different conversation depending on his age. By the time he gets into middle and high school, more than likely he has heard about sex from more than one person. Teach your son that it's okay if he chooses to be abstinent. Encourage him not to fall for peer pressure from his friends and others. Help him understand what he would be getting himself into and speak to him about the benefits of being abstinent. Don't be too holy to talk about sex. If you find that you can't properly get the important details across, share with your son sex education books or videos (there are good ones on YouTube; just be sure to watch them first to ensure that they align with thc message that you want to convey).

Remind him that it is perfectly okay to say "no" to others including his girlfriend. I, too, felt pressured to have sex with women in the past, especially in college. Peer pressure is everywhere. Being pressured or shamed into having sex is tough when you have no one to turn to for advice. I found myself doing things that I wouldn't have done if I would've had sound advice. You have a chance to become the mom, grandmother, aunt, sister, or cousin that he needs. Be honest and informative and help guide your son to be able to sustain a healthy relationship.

If he is abstaining from sex, reassure him that although his choice may not be that popular with his friends at school, it could save him many headaches and emotional pain in his future. Make sure that he is aware that being sexually active can lead to contracting sexually transmitted diseases, unwanted pregnancies as well as developing exhausting emotional attachments. His choices will define his future. Explain to him through your stories and the stories of others you know how having an unplanned child can derail his future. Teach him to be more deliberate and thoughtful with his choices. If you didn't make all the right choices regarding sex, be transparent with him. Not only will it bring the two of you closer, but your experiences can also be a cautionary tale. Share with your son what can happen if he moves too fast, doesn't think through choices, and is negatively influenced by the people around him.

At age eleven or twelve, as he goes through puberty, his hormones will sometimes become overwhelming for him. He could have swelling of the testicles because he will be developing and storing sperm in his scrotum sacs. His hormones could cause him to come across as angry, but he is trying to cope with the changes he is currently experiencing. He may have erections for no reason at all and not understand why or become embarrassed. If you witness it, don't bring attention to it. It will embarrass him further.

According to the article, "Concerns Boys Have About Puberty," "Boys have pubertal concerns and worries, too, including the following: Young men go through voice changes, wet dreams, involuntary erections, breast enlargement and one testicle lower than the other." A wet dream doesn't mean you had a sexual dream. Boys wake up with semen in their underwear. This is a part of growing up. Parents should explain this to their sons and not make a big deal. Erections can happen at any time. Your son doesn't have to be thinking about sex. Let him know it's okay.

It can be embarrassing to have an erection in public. I was in class one day in 4th grade and the teacher called me to the board, but I had an erection before she called me up. She thought I was being disobedient and scolded me for not going to the board. The real reason was I didn't want the embarrassment of standing up and being laughed at by classmates for having an erection.

The article goes on to say, "As your child approaches and enters puberty, be sensitive to his need for privacy. Preteens often become more modest while they bathe or change their clothes. Respect this wish for privacy, not only as it relates to their bodies but in other areas as well, such as remembering to knock before entering their rooms. Preteens also become more sensitive about how they look during this time. Their interest in grooming increases and they are frequently concerned with their appearance, thanks largely to influence from their peers and advertising messages. Watch for signs of a child who has a negative image of their bodies, which in some cases can result in an eating disorder." Puberty brings about so many different changes in the body mentally and physically. Be sensitive to this. Limit the jokes about it and give your son privacy when he needs it. It will allow him to experience puberty with less stress.

If you've already discussed abstinence, talk to him about the importance of using condoms if he finds himself in a situation where he has decided to move forward. Demonstrate how to use a condom by using a banana. You might feel uncomfortable doing this but it's a good example and he needs to know how to use it. Optionally, you could share an online video with him. If you don't explain to him how to use one, he may not use one at all or he may use it improperly, defeating the purpose. If you're not ready to be a grandmother, the thought of taking care of your young son's child may help see you through.

There are several videos available demonstrating how to properly use a condom. Go on YouTube to pick videos you are comfortable with. According to *Better Condom Education for High School Students: Putting Data into Practice,* when they asked students about the ways they were using condoms, "Seven in 10 reported they did not squeeze the tip of the condom before putting it on. Half reported that they did not hold the base of the penis when pulling out." According to these statistics, most young men are not using condoms correctly which can lead to unwanted pregnancies, diseases and discomfort. I taught my son the proper way to use a condom by using a banana to demonstrate how to put a condom on. This was very effective because I had him practice how to use one several times. Another method is to have 4 steps on cards and do trivia with your son how to put the 4 cards in chronological order for proper use of a condom.

Speak to your son about the emotions involved with sex for a man and a woman. If he is involved or strongly considering being sexually involved, help him to understand that the young woman that he wants to connect with is giving her body to him and that in most cases she is also giving him her heart. Many young men don't realize nor understand just how serious sex can be for some young ladies. Share with him how most young ladies feel about sex, especially when it is with a young man that she deeply cares about. Help him to understand that there is a spiritual attachment that comes with sex, that should not be ignored. Explain to him that in some religions sex is what consummates a marriage. Help him acknowledge that when he has sex with a young lady, there are responsibilities that come along with it; be they emotions, pregnancy, or disease. He cannot run from the results of their union.

Discuss with your son the emotional journey you went through after becoming sexually involved. Share with him what your concerns were when you lost your virginity. Explain to him why you chose to have sex when you did. Let him know if you felt pressured. Share with him what you wish your partner knew about how he made you feel if he moved too fast. Be candid about your early experiences in terms of if your first sexual encounter was with your husband, boyfriend, friend or some random guy you barely knew. Explain to him the emotional damage that may have taken place due to someone moving too fast, being too aggressive, being selfish, or abandoning you. Let him know if you have regrets. On the other hand, if your first sexual encounter was positive, share what made if right for you. If it was because you waited until you knew that your partner loved you, let him know that. If it was because you waited until you got married, share that as well. Share this information with your son. Once you have had the much-needed conversation, help him to see the parallels that could take place in his own relationships.

Your Son's First Girlfriend

In a world where social media is a place to connect with "friends," many kids meet on the internet not knowing much of anything about each other. They see a young lady at a social event or at school and want to date her. Some of them get into sexual relationships before they get to know each other. Your son will start dating at some point, whether you agree with it or not, but you can advocate that he should never date a young lady he hasn't been friends with first. Coaching him is essential to his ability to foster a healthy relationship. Fifteen or sixteen years old is a good age to begin dating, but building friendships first gives them both the opportunity to know each other better.

How will you know if he is dating the right person? You won't. You will only know the values you have instilled in him. When your son begins dating a young lady, it would be in your best interest to get to know her also. If you remain objective, you'll have a better idea of who she really is.

During the "friends first" phase, red flags tend to appear. If your son is friends with the young lady first, he hopefully will notice these flags and will have time to decide if he wants to pursue something more serious or remain friends. If she starts doing inappropriate things, or your son finds out that she is not the kind of person he wants to be with, it will not be as tough to cut ties with her because they have not crossed any sexual boundaries or professed their love for one another.

The goal is for your son to learn what to do and what not to do during the "friends first" and dating phases. If your son dates in high school, he will know what to expect when he gets to college. He may go off track and make a mistake, but his instincts should kick in. If not, he will either learn the lesson or repeat the mistakes until he gets it. There are different phases that young men should experience while dating. If he can get the dating phase right, he will have a smooth transition into a healthier, stronger, long-term relationship. Your son is also watching how you engage with his father, his stepfather or your boyfriend. If you became friends with your partner before you dated, or you got right into dating, or right into bed for that matter, he will take his cues from you.

The relationship between your son and his first girlfriend is so sensitive and so important to understand. His first girlfriend is everything to him. He is smitten, while experiencing a deep emotional connection that feels different from any relationship that he has ever had. Tread lightly on this one because your son might feel like he has feelings for her that are deeper than they really are. Observe the situation, listen, and ask him positive, calculated questions like, "How long have you known each other?" "What is your definition of a healthy relationship?" "How do you feel about long-distance dating?" "What is your definition of being in love?" "Can you see yourself exclusively with this young lady?" "Do you know who her ex-boyfriend(s) are and are they still friends?" "Why did they break up?" "Have you met her parents?" "Do you know where she lives?" "What is important to her and does that line up with your priorities?" Allow your son to answer in detail. Understand that he is just now experiencing eros, or romantic love. He doesn't fully understand what love is. This is a whole new experience, and he will have so much to learn. Be there to guide him.

Summer camps were fun when I was a kid. I'd go to camp for one or two weeks, meet a young lady, ask her to be my girlfriend. We would be a couple for the duration of the time at camp, then return home and never see each other again, but I did think of her from time to time. But for those one or two weeks, I felt like I was in love and had the girl of my dreams.

When your son asks for advice about what to do concerning his crush, you must choose your answers and how you react wisely because if your reaction is too negative, he may never ask you again. Be sure not to belittle him or make him feel silly for his feelings. Doing so will only push him into secrecy. After all your experiences in real adult relationships, your son's crush may seem meaningless to you, but it means the world to him.

On the other hand, don't just force your will or input on his relationship without being invited in. If he asks for your advice, it's because he trusts you. To find out how serious his crush is, be an active listener. Talk to him about his feelings toward this young lady to find out where his head is. Find out what he likes about her and what makes her so special to him. Allow him to go into detail about the situation so that you know how to advise him moving forward.

If he decides to pursue her, teach your son to give the young lady space by doing everything concerning her in moderation. A girl wants to know a guy is interested, but she doesn't want to feel smothered. That's not dating. That's called stalking. All jokes aside, coach him not to move too quickly. Let him know that you understand that when you have a strong interest in someone that it is hard to get them out of your mind. Tell him you understand that he may feel like he is in love, but he should slow down, continuing to pursue, but not overdoing. Teach him not to love anybody or anything more than he loves God and himself.

Your Son's Girlfriend Spending the Night

If you have a son who is eighteen or older, you might be faced with the question of allowing his girlfriend to stay the night at your house at some point. I've heard of situations where this issue has come up, even when the young man was in high school. So, is it okay for your son's girlfriend to spend the night? Unless they are engaged and about to be married, the answer is, "absolutely not." You will be sending a bad message when you allow your son to have his lady friend spend the night. More than likely, he will eventually have other women in his life. He may have several. Will all of them be allowed to spend the night? Not if you want to establish respect for your household. If that's the case, boundaries must be set in your home; your son just can't do what he wants whenever he wants to do it. This will result in a lack of discipline, accountability and a lack of boundaries, which can contribute to why many young men are disrespectful to young ladies and their own mothers. Using your home as a hotel shouldn't be an option. I have heard some mothers say they would rather their sons have sex in their house than somewhere else. This is a horrible excuse to justify your sons' behavior. Your son will respect you more if you set boundaries.

Some parents think it's okay for their son's girlfriend to spend the night when they are in high school. My mother never allowed any girls to spend the night at our house when I was in high school. She only allowed my serious girlfriend in college to spend the night at our house. I strongly disagree with allowing a son's high school girlfriend to spend the night in his parents' home. I have several reasons for this. One, high schoolers are too young and too immature. Two, it is irresponsible for adults to allow it to take place. If a young lady gets pregnant it would happen on your watch at your home, which makes you partly responsible. Lastly, it would send your son the wrong message about respecting himself, your home and the women he dates. Most high school students never marry their high school sweetheart, but it does happen in some cases. If so, they have plenty of time to be together in their own place once they can afford it. Saying, "no," teaches respect, discipline, perseverance and patience to your child. College is another discussion.

Some mothers want to build trust with their sons, so they are a little more lenient with their sons bringing home girlfriends. Some mothers may argue that their son is in college and making good grades. For example, winter break is coming so he wants to spend time with his girlfriend and asks to bring her home. By agreeing to this, understand the ramifications that can follow. If it is a holiday or special occasion and your son wants to bring his college girlfriend home to participate, allowing them to sleep in separate rooms is the best solution. If there is not space to do so, put your son on the couch while she takes his room. They may not be happy with the arrangement, but they will have to respect your decision if he wants her home for the holidays.

How To Handle Your Son's Breakup

Losing a friend or significant other can be one of the toughest things for a young person. I remember being in sixth grade and liking a young lady. One Monday afternoon, I walked into the cafeteria and spotted her sitting with her friends, so I strolled over and gave her half the penny candy I'd just bought with my last fifty cents. She was happy and her friends were smiling. She hugged me and kissed me on the cheek. My day was made. I don't remember walking to class after that. I think I floated.

On Wednesday of that same week, she walked up to me and broke up with me in front of my friends. I was confused. I can laugh about it today, but as a 10-year-old kid, I was hurt. I didn't even know what love was, but I knew I was hurting. I really liked her and didn't understand how you could be floating on clouds one day and in the dumps shortly after that. I never got an explanation for the breakup. Maybe that would have brought me closure, instead I was left in the dark.

Emotions in young men start early. I recall recognizing my emotions in sixth grade, but I didn't know how to handle them. I was clueless about relationships because no one had spoken to me about them. When people say women are from Venus and men are from Mars, that is a real comparison. Men and women don't understand certain aspects of each other, even as adults. I never told my mother what happened with the young lady because I didn't think she would understand. Instead, I tried to figure it out on my own. I even asked a few of my friends for advice, but that wasn't a good decision either. I walked around for a few days looking sad at the advice of my friends, but that made me look pitiful and helpless. She and her friends laughed at me. I was embarrassed and wished I had never taken their advice. My so-called friends also laughed after I acted out on their advice. How ironic. Eventually, life went on. It's funny now, but I was so tarnished by that incident that I don't think I ever bought candy for anyone else again until I was in high school.

When your son is in a serious relationship later in life, the short relationships he had back in the past will affect his thought process. He will be more cautious handling situations. Hurt is hurt, whether it happens to a child or a grown man.

Tips for Mothers to be Supportive of Sons in Relationships

1. Handle your son's relationships with empathy. Be a good listener. Respond at the right time.

2. Tell your son stories about your first love or first relationship. He needs to know the good, the bad and what you learned from it.

3. Help your son understand women and how they think from your perspective, so he gains a better understanding of their thought process.

4. Let your son know that you care about his relationships and want to help and he can come to you if need be. This will go a long way with him.

5. Probe periodically but listen when he is ready to talk and allow your son to express himself fully.

6. Explain the ups and downs of relationships to your son. Let him know that some days will be better than others, but if he experiences disappointment in a relationship, he will make it through.

7. Let your son know that expressing his emotions is healthy, but only to the right person. Be that person for him by creating a safe environment for him to do so.

8. Let your son know that the best relationship to have until he is mature enough to properly navigate his feelings and hers, is the one with himself and God.

Your son needs to know that healthy relationships grow and have different stages. Some people will only be in his life for a season. However, a full-grown, healthy relationship will follow the following path:

Steps to a Healthy Relationship

1. **Start as friends.** Get to know each other as people.

2. **Date.** Hanging out with each other will show him a lot about the other person. It also gives him time to see if this is who he wants to commit to.

3. **Commit to a Relationship.** Committing to a relationship verbally, or with a promise ring, signifies that he wants to spend his life with her. It tells the other person that he doesn't want anyone else but her, but that there is still work to be done before they commit to marriage.

4. **Get engaged.** He knows beyond a shadow of a doubt that this is the person he wants to spend the rest of his life with, so he asks her to marry him and they begin preparation for the wedding and a life together.

5. **Get married.** Marriage is supposed to be a life-long commitment. Your son should not do it unless he is 100% sure. This is when the real work begins. Getting married doesn't mean a person stops dating. It means that two people have committed to building their lives and their legacy together.

6. **Have children.** Some people have kids and then get married. However, if marriage comes first, then they have time to enjoy their new covenant and get to learn about each other in marriage before bringing in another life.

7. **Bonus: Keep dating.** When he gets married, he must continue to date his spouse. It is so important for him and his wife to find time to enjoy each other and remember why they fell in love with each other and decided to get married in the first place.

The phases of a healthy, romantic relationship are meant to build a man's capacity to learn, listen and love the right way. When two people become friends, it allows them to witness someone at their best and their worst without the emotional commitment. When two people date, it gives them an opportunity to develop feelings for each other beyond friendship. If it feels too awkward, it's never too late to turn back. Some people are better off in the friend zone. A promise ring is a statement of love and commitment even though both people know they need to work on themselves before making a lifelong commitment. Getting engaged and married should happen after discovering that despite each other's shortcomings, they choose to love one another unconditionally and can see themselves building a future together. Many people who are currently married dated off and on before they tied the knot because they weren't sure. It is better to put time and thought into such a major step to better ensure longevity and compatibility.

Having children is a blessing but it changes relationships. You are no longer responsible for only yourselves. You now have a full-time job of taking care of a child. If the relationship is not strong, kids will not necessarily help build it. They can bring more strain. Dating after marriage is important because dating is what led the two of you to tie the knot in the first place. Also, dating allows you to get a small break from the stress of parenting and allow you to reacquaint with the each other outside of the children.

Encourage Healthy Relationships

Encourage your son to build healthy relationships. A healthy relationship looks like this: Two people talking, getting along with each other and enjoying one another's company. They talk about their futures and interests. They set goals and objectives for themselves and as a couple. They treat each other with love, respect, trust, honesty, fairness, support, accountability and safety. They live in peace and harmony, not in stress and strife. Neither is perfect, but both work to be better versions of themselves.

Healthy relationships start with self-respect and they require that you love yourself before you love anyone else. Encourage your son to treat himself with respect. Urge him not to abuse his body with drugs or alcohol and to eliminate stress in his life. Explain to him that an unhealthy relationship is evident by him and his significant other being more stressed with each other than happy daily. People often fall in love quickly only to find out over time that the relationship is toxic and unhealthy.

Toxic relationships are led by negative emotions. At least one of the committed is always obsessing over what the other person is doing. If your son is the toxic person in the relationship, it means he manipulates the other person and maybe even their friends, pretending he is sincere when he really is not. Your son needs to understand that it could also be the other person who has hidden motives. This becomes evident when he finds out that she is talking behind his back to other people in their circle, if she becomes jealous when he speaks to or hangs out with others, or doesn't want him to have friends. Controlling, toxic people forcibly invite themselves to their significant other's home or events and functions they're not invited to.

Be it verbal, physical or emotional abuse, a toxic person has uncontrollable emotions and actions and will cause the relationship to remain unhealthy. Help your son to understand that if he possesses any of these traits that he will be harmful to any relationship. Verbal abuse is when someone uses their words to humiliate you. They degrade you or belittle you to make you feel worthless, reducing you to a lower position through embarrassment and shame. Physical abuse includes pushing, shoving, smacking, kicking, hitting or holding tightly. Emotional abuse is when someone needs to know where you are always, even driving by your job or home, checking to make sure you are where you say you are. These people control what you wear by telling you what they want to see you in or how you should wear your hair.

Your son should never exhibit or tolerate this type of behavior. Controlling himself and his own thoughts is tough. However, self-control is the best control to have. Let him know it's okay to walk away if things aren't working out in a relationship, especially if he and his girlfriend are arguing every day. If she makes the choice to walk away or feels like he is too much for her and she needs some air, it's also okay. He needs to grasp that if he and she cannot come together on the smallest issues, it means that the two of them need to work on themselves apart from the relationship. He should use the time productively and focus on building himself.

Share with him that allowing an overbearing girlfriend to remain in his life shows that he doesn't love himself. Being overbearing means he doesn't love himself or her. No one should be controlling what another person wears, how they walk, who they talk to or where they go. If the other person gets angry for the other standing up for themself, it is apparent that they are not someone to build a relationship with. No one deserves to be treated that way by anyone.

Teenagers witness more unhealthy relationships than they care to talk about. Don't be afraid to discuss with your son healthy versus unhealthy relationships. Share some of your experiences and those of others you know. They can be used as examples for him of what not to do. We all have regretted dating someone and have learned from a dysfunctional relationship. Don't live the rest of your life in shame about your mistakes. Let them be cautionary tales for your son.

Healthy relationships, on the other hand, are built on respect, trust, honesty, good communication, compromise, empathy, patience and fairness. These are the principles we should all stand by in our own personal relationships. A relationship missing one of these attributes can become toxic. All relationships go through peaks and valleys. Even healthy relationships. However, overall relationships should carry positive vibes and synergy. Peace is paramount and should be the place that the relationship steers toward. If the relationship is more stressful than peaceful, it is not healthy.

If your son plays sports in high school and has plans to continue in college, he will definitely be in a long-term relationship with the sport he plays. I spent more time at practice, working out and in film sessions in college than I ever did in high school because the game changed and became more time-sensitive. It was a productive way for me to spend my time. If your son is not an athlete, encourage him to get involved in something in high school and college. Idle time is the enemy. Hobbies, clubs, organizations and sports often help to shape an individual's identity and character. In tough times such as after breakups, having extra-curricular activities to participate in can help them to shift their focus from the pain.

Mothers, it is imperative that you allow your son to connect with women outside of you and the women in your family, without your interference. It is important to understand that your son's life is his own. Whether you like it or not, your son will make choices that appeal to his thought process and his needs, not yours. If you choose to be possessive, not only will you run the women in his life away, but you'll also create a wedge between you and your son. Being judgmental, jealous, and insecure about his romantic relationships is not only unhealthy for your son and his relationships, but for his relationship with you as well.

Respect the Woman He Chooses

A mother wants her son to choose the right woman, but sometimes it doesn't happen that way. Regardless of whether you think his girlfriend is good for him or not, he chose her. Although you may have several choice thoughts about her, keep your opinions to yourself. Show respect to your son by picking your words wisely. Also, talking to other people about her while she's around is not cool and could potentially drive a wedge between you and your son. Further, body language is stronger than words. Your negative feelings about your son's girlfriend show without you ever murmuring a word. Control your body language when your son's lady is in your presence. Respect his decision and do your best to keep the peace.

When it comes to women, other women often notice red flags quicker than men do. Men are visual creatures, so they only see with their eyes in the beginning. Your son's intuition may not be as keen as yours, so the woman he likes may be unattractive to you but gorgeous to him. You may have a problem with her personality, but he may love it. However, if you try to interfere in his relationship with this young lady, you could inadvertently damage your relationship with him. Your son wants to make his own choices. Your actions might cause him to choose her over you.

When your son knows that you don't like the woman he's in love with, he may suddenly disappear for days or weeks. If he knows, she likely knows it too and won't want to come around. He may feel pushed into a corner and want to avoid any trouble with his lady. If he's married and must make a choice between his mom and his wife, you may not be pleased with his decision. If you want to maintain a relationship with your son, don't go down that road. Genesis 2:24 reads "a man leaves his father and mother and is united to his wife, and they become one flesh." "One flesh" doesn't include you. According to Proverbs 18:22, "He who finds a wife finds what is good and receives favor from the Lord." It doesn't say that a man who finds a "mother" finds a good thing. This isn't to say that you're not a good thing, but your son will and is supposed to cleave to his wife.

This is difficult for some mothers to hear, but you can also use this young lady as an advocate for you to build a stronger relationship with him. Take her out to lunch or to the spa. Ask her meaningful questions about herself and her family. Get to know her. If she likes you, she'll advocate to your son on your behalf. When your son's significant other truly enjoys your company, the odds of you being incorporated in your son's family's dynamics increase. If she likes being around you, she'll make sure that she, your son and their children (if they have them) visit you often or send for you to visit with them. She may ensure that you receive nice gifts for your birthday, Mother's Day, and other special occasions. Become an ally instead of an enemy of your son's significant other.

Your Son's Standards and Choices

You are your son's first example of a woman. He has watched your interactions with your husband or significant other and took mental notes based on what he saw. If you were loving and caring, there is a great chance that he will seek the same kind of woman. A spiteful, short-tempered and abrasive upbringing could possibly cause him to unconsciously gravitate to someone who is similar. If he despises the pain that kind of temperament causes, he'll deliberately choose someone who is opposite you.

Finding the right woman will be based on your son's standards and mindset. It is all about timing and he must be in the right mind space to welcome someone into his life long term. Age is a major factor. When he is younger, he really doesn't know what he wants. After experiencing a few relationships, there is a good chance he'll figure out exactly what he is looking for and what he wants to avoid in a long-term relationship. He will learn that there are phases to a healthy relationship (whether he chooses to follow them or not): friendship, dating, engagement, then marriage and finally children. Many of us didn't follow the model because we didn't understand the importance of it, so we can't always expect our son to. We can only encourage him, but not force him.

If you take the time to teach him what to look for in a potential partner, instead of allowing him to be solely influenced by what he sees on TV about dating, you can feel at ease about your son's love life. Celebrities are not always good examples. Teach him about healthy relationships through your transparency. If he is equipped with an understanding of relationships, their purpose and how they should work, you should be at ease about letting him go. If you can loosen your grip, not only will he not have to choose between his girlfriend or his mom, but he will be wiser in his decision making.

Find out why he chose the young lady. Ask questions such as: What do you like about her? What does she want to do with her life? Has she been married and does she have children? What are her family dynamics like? Who has she dated in the past? What does she like most about you? Keep it light and speak in a light-hearted and easy manner. Even when you give your son advice, he will make his own observations and choices. You cannot choose his mate for him, but you can position him to make a sound choice.

Your son's standards may be different from yours. You have a picture of the ideal woman for your son in mind but more than likely, he holds a very different image. When he does decide to get into a serious relationship with the wrong person, you may see the signs before anyone else. You may see and feel disrespectful energy from a young lady even when your son doesn't. You may see her lack of motivation. This can be very frustrating to watch, especially when his girlfriend is a negative influence on him.

When you know that the woman your son is with is not right for him, go to him with facts and allow him to decide how he will move forward. Maybe your son didn't start smoking and drinking until he met her; maybe his grades dropped when he met her; maybe he picked up bad habits from her. Maintain your composure if you are ready to do bodily harm to her. Don't go to his girlfriend to "speak your piece." No young man wants his mom approaching his girlfriend about their relationship; it makes him look weak, incapable and like a Mama's boy. It's better to let your son know you're disappointed, but don't yell and fuss or get into an altercation with him when you speak with him. He will only focus on your emotions, not the content of your concerns. Life's biggest lessons are learned from experiences. Allow him to go through the experience and learn the lesson. There is also a chance that your son and his significant other will work through their issues and grow from them. If you choose to get involved and insert yourself in the middle of your son's messy relationship and they work it out, you lose because they will have moved on and grown closer. You, however, will have caused unnecessary damage to your relationship with both of them that will take some time to repair.

Prepare Your Son to Date

It is your job to make sure your son is prepared to date. Make it a priority to discuss dating with him. Share with him what a healthy relationship looks like. If you are not sure what a healthy relationship looks like because you haven't experienced one, tell him what an unhealthy and dysfunctional relationship looks like and encourage him to seek the opposite. Your son needs to hear about relationships from a woman's perspective, particularly yours. Discuss the choices you've made good and bad. Describe what was a successful time in the relationship and what felt dysfunctional. Tell him to watch for red flags, even when he is young and may not know the difference between good and bad signs when dating.

I knew nothing about dating because my mom and I never discussed it, but I wish we had. In fact, most of my friends learned about dating from friends. It was like the blind leading the blind. I wished my mother had given me even a little bit of insight. I had to learn so much on my own. I got wrong information and made plenty of mistakes. I believe that I would have been better in relationships if we had discussed it. Help your son determine what is important when choosing someone to connect with. He may have a list of preferences but encourage him to look deeper than the usual line items, like pretty, long hair and small waist. Help him to dig deeper into the characteristics that would mesh well with his personality. For example, help him to see what is important to him, be it someone who has a good sense of humor or is really laid back, someone who is intelligent or creative, someone who is softspoken or outspoken, someone who loves God first or has a strong connection to her ancestors. Share with him the importance of finding a virtuous woman, or someone who is honest, trustworthy, thoughtful, has good energy and who communicates well. Suggest that he ask himself, *If I wasn't attracted to her physical appearance, would I want her to be my friend?*

You are No Longer the #1 Woman in His Life

You will always have a special place in your son's heart. You carried him for nine months. Your son will always love you, even if you made mistakes along the way. If you are his biological or adopted mom, you changed his diapers, fed him and lost sleep taking care of him. If you are a relative that became his caretaker, you also sacrificed your time and energy to raise him. Whatever the case may be, you and your son may have had a close relationship for many years. You may have attended ball games, musical concerts, academic competitions, graduation, visited him in college and sent care packages. Those memories are stored in the back of your mind and his. Then one day, he grows up and meets his Miss Right. Picture this: he can't concentrate because he thinks about her day and night. He used to call you every day, but now you may get a call once a week. He wants to bring her home to meet "Mom." She's not like the rest of girls he has dated. He never introduced any of them to you, so you know she is special and he is serious about this one.

Your son's past relationships didn't last long, but this relationship has endured and is far from casual. Maybe they go to church together and she attends family functions. He took a trip to the beach with her. Maybe he has flooded his social media pages with pictures with her. (You know that men don't post women on their social media page unless the relationship is serious.) This relationship is serious! No need to panic if you have prepared him for this moment. No need to worry about her taking your place because she never will. However, she will occupy a different space in his life and I suggest you move over and help make room for her.

When your son gets into a serious, monogamous relationship or decides to get married, you will no longer be the number one woman in his life. This is difficult for some mothers to understand, especially single mothers. In a lot of cases, your son is so much more to you; he has fulfilled an emotional attachment in your life. But as sons mature into men, their needs and desires change, while some mothers want and feel like they need them to remain the same. Dorothy Tennov coined the word limerence in 1977 as a "state of being infatuated or obsessed with another person, typically experienced involuntarily, and characterized by a strong desire for reciprocation of one's feelings but not primarily for a sexual relationship." This is what happens in many mother-son relationships.

When I was single, I went out to dinner with my mom often and had Sunday dinners at her house from time to time. When I got married, all that changed (not to mention my eating habits changed, and my mom had a tough time with that). She was used to me eating the fried foods and cakes she made, but, as I got older, I cut back on eating so many sweets and fried foods. I had a different schedule with varying responsibilities. I couldn't make it to all the Sunday dinners and my mom was in her feelings about it. She told me that I'd changed and she was right. I couldn't continue to eat certain foods because I wanted my weight and good health to remain intact. I could handle it when I was younger, but my body had changed with age.

My mother believed my wife had an influence on me that directly impacted my eating habits. She was right. My wife did have an influence on me and I had an influence on her. She taught me how to eat healthier. I reminded my mother that my wife made dinner for me, just like my mom did for her ex-husband. In fact, when my mom was still with her ex, she wasn't involved in my life as much. She was always with him, which was fine with me. He was her husband.

A shift takes place when your son gets married. You must adjust. Understand that his wife is the woman he chose to share his life with and plans to grow old with. Take that seriously. If you show her disrespect, she will see that you don't care for her and find a way to shut you out of their lives.

Some mothers will make statements like, "This is my son's house," "I know what my baby likes," or compliment your son on something new or nice in his house knowing full well that his wife put it there. Other mothers might belittle the words or actions of their sons' romantic partner, becoming isolating, ignoring them, while making no attempt to get to know them. Some mothers may become mean-spirited and advocate for their son to leave the young lady for no reason, without facts or evidence of her wrongdoing. This blatant disrespect and disregard are a recipe for a broken relationship with both her and with your son. You don't want to be a foe to your son's wife. That is an immature approach. Furthermore, you don't want your relationship with your son's lady to become a competition for his affection.

Your son and his wife or girlfriend unite as one every time they are intimate with each other. She has influence over him and according to the bible he and his wife are becoming one flesh. Don't feel threatened by this. Change your thought process and interject positive energy into their relationship. Support them with the hope that they will find success in their union. Look at it differently. Do you want your son to have a failed marriage? Would you prefer that he runs through women and commit to none? Would you prefer that he has all of his children with one person or have numerous baby mamas all over town? When your son commits to one woman look at it as a victory. You are not losing a son, but you are gaining a daughter if you properly handle the transition.

My situation with my mother was not as strong as other situations I've seen, however, there was some turbulence when she first met my wife to be. My mother didn't acknowledge her in the beginning of our relationship because for the first time in quite some time it had become clear that I was serious. At the time, my wife and I were dating and getting to know each other. It was fresh, but we were spending a lot of time together, which took away from some of the time that I would have normally spent with my mom when I was single. I took my girlfriend to a family function at my sister's house and introduced her to some of my family. She hugged each of my sisters, but when she got to my mother and attempted to hug her, my mom frowned and jerked away, rejecting the embrace. She had never met my girlfriend, never had a conversation with her, didn't know anything about her character, so there was no reason for such a reaction. My future wife was shocked and offended. This one action defined the tone of their relationship for quite some time. My girlfriend felt uncomfortable anytime she was around my mother from that point forward and it put a speed bump in the progress of our relationship. Her behavior toward my wife was personal and there was no excuse for it.

Fortunately, with time, my mother and wife were able to come to repair their relationship, but others are not so fortunate. Understandably, mothers are going to move more cautiously than their sons. Every mother wants their son to find the right match. However, you'll never know if she is truly the right match if you never give her a chance.

After marriage, the order is God, wife, children, then everyone else. You are in the "everyone else" category, but you are still special. If remaining relevant with your son is a concern for you, during the natural course of his marriage your presence will be lifesaving or at least a much-needed mental break from the pressures of parenthood. When they start having babies, they will need your assistance. If the relationship with you is not solid, you will miss out on watching and being a part of your grandchildren growing up. Being a steadfast grandmother to your grandchildren and helping them out on date night will go a long way. Practice healthy distancing, play it cool and allow your son and his wife to live their lives and they will call on you often and appreciate your willingness to help them out.

Pushing Your Dreams on Your Son

There are numerous examples of mothers wanting one thing for their sons, while he has different aspirations for himself. Mothers are concerned about their sons' career goals, future residency, college options and other lifestyle choices. When those aspirations line up with their sons' wishes, everything tends to work out. However, when those wishes clash, chaos ensues between mother and son which could lead to disappointments, disagreements, and frustration on both parts. Your son could become rebellious and make bad choices. The conflict of vision can even damage your relationship.

Your reasons for your dreams for your son can vary widely as well. One reason could be living vicariously through him. If you didn't get to accomplish your dream of, say going to medical school and becoming a doctor because you became pregnant and your priorities had to change, you may want your son to take the baton and become a doctor. You could want him to be a professional athlete because it seems like he'll make a lot of money and gain fame or you'll get to go to all his games and become social media famous for being his mother. Another reason could be that your family has a long history of holding respectable, professional careers, so you want your son to follow in those footsteps. It may just be a practical thought about his choices as related to finances that determines your thought process. For example, if your son wants to go to college in a different part of the country, you may be concerned about out-of-state tuition, him being so far away and you not being able to see him as much or the cost of him traveling back and forth between semesters. The list goes on. Whatever the thought process is, the problem with those varied scenarios is that none of the reasons have anything to do with your son's wants and aspirations for himself. They are all about you and what you want for him.

He might not want to become a doctor but wants to start his own business. He may not want to become a professional athlete; he may prefer to play an instrument or play chess and grow up to live a low-key life, absent of fans and a hectic lifestyle. He may not want the stuffiness and responsibility of a professional career. He may have a more creative nature and want to become an artist, singer or actor. Regarding relocating far away for school, he might just want a change of atmosphere, a new experience. There are financial options for out-of-state tuition that he could explore. As much as it could go against everything that you may envision for your son's future, you must allow him to live his own life.

Pushing your choices for your son's future can cause him to resent you later in life. Doing so forces him to abandon his own desires for himself. God made each of us different with our own unique set of wants, needs, desires and thought processes. Instead of willing your desires on your son, take the time to observe him. What are the things that come easy for him? For example, if he was interested in dinosaurs when he was a kid and continues to be fascinated by them, maybe he would do well to explore becoming a paleontologist. If he watches you closely in the kitchen and has a natural curiosity for how different foods are prepared, or how different spices affect the outcome of the taste of different foods, culinary arts may be his forte. If your son loves the stars and the universe, maybe he should consider pursuing astronomy. If he excels in math, maybe he could teach algebra or geometry at a school or work at a bank. If he runs his own lemonade stand, cuts grass or shovels snow, maybe he should pursue entrepreneurship. If he is an excellent writer, maybe he should be an author or journalist and write books or contribute to magazine and newspapers. If your son excels in sports, let him play as long as he enjoys it and can.

There are always signs. It is your job as his mother to take note and to help him become aware of his natural inclinations. Help him nurture his abilities. Find schools, programs, books and other resources to help him grow and excel in the field that calls him. Every child is good at something, but it takes patience to find out what that something is. Sit down with him and explore college options that make sense for his career choice. Working together allows you both to be involved. Teach him to be true to himself and to ask pertinent questions of himself, like the following: "Do I think I'll enjoy doing this 10 years from now?" "Will this career provide the kind of income that I desire for myself?" "What is the education route to take to be able to enter into this field?" "What kinds of internships are available in this field?" "What would be the best city to live in to be successful in my chosen field?" "How long will it take to get the credentials I need to begin working in this field?" There is so much to consider. Research and assistance from you and a guidance counselor will help him make informed, relevant decisions for his future. But remember that the ultimate decision has to be up to him.

It is also important that you speak positive words into your son as he is preparing for his future. Let him know that you believe in him. Encourage him to trust the plan that he has created for himself knowing that if it has to change for whatever unforeseen reason, that it is not a death sentence. Let him know that it is okay and remind him that he is capable of regrouping and revising his plan. Tell him that he is equipped with everything that he needs to be successful. Allow him to go out and explore and to ultimately make his own choices and to learn from his experiences. That is what life is all about. In order for him to grow, you must let him go.

My son is a Morehouse College graduate. When he was young, he had open-heart surgery. As long as I can remember he has always wanted to be a surgeon. My wife and I encouraged him in his academics and he was in all-honors classes in high school. He majored in Biology while he was in college. We thought he was going to start applying to medical schools because that was his plan. Instead, his life took a turn. He met a young lady and fell in love. I found out that I was going to be a grandfather before he graduated from college. When my son told me that I was going to be a grandfather, I was shocked and disappointed, but happy at the same time. All the work my wife and I put in over the years changed overnight and his plans of being a surgeon changed. This scenario was never a consideration when we talked about his future. It was never even a worry because of how conservative my son is by nature. However, his life plan changed drastically and quickly.

My wife and I had worked with our son his whole life to help him pursue his goal of becoming a surgeon. We helped him raise money for college through the Beautillion program. We supported him through college so that he could focus on his studies. He did well. Only now, his focus has changed. He and his girlfriend now have two children. We would prefer that they be married, but they want to wait. His life looks nothing like what we envisioned, but it is okay because it is his life to be lived by him. Our job is to advise him in the way that he should go. It may take him longer to build his wealth than what we'd hoped for, but it is his journey to be had. This was a tough pill for both my wife and I to swallow, but we understand that we can't make decisions for him. His choices define his future and we have learned to step back to let him make his own decisions. I wanted one thing for him. I thought we were on the same page, but he chose another route. However, he is healthy and happy and is building a family, maybe not in the order that I would prefer, but in a way that works for him and his girlfriend.

It will be interesting to see where he lands. He is a smart young man. He is an adult and I have taught him in the way in which he should go, now I have let go and trust that everything that I have taught him will come into play and shape the ultimate outcome. If he asks me for assistance, I will give it to him. His life choices are his, not mine. The same goes for you and your son. The twists and turns in life will lead him to his purpose.

Teach Your Son His Purpose

Your purpose is your calling in life. According to Ephesians 2:10, "He also has a specific purpose for each of us that is His unique, tailor-made plan for our individual life."

Every person, young and old wants to know where they come from, including who their mom and dad are, family history, how they got their names and more importantly, what their purpose is in life. It is vital that your son gets to know himself and becomes fine with who he is. Every person is born with unique gifts, talents and traits. Although most kids and adults don't know their purpose, you can give your son an advantage if you help him find his or at the very least teach him the process of finding his purpose. A good place to start is *The Purpose Driven Life* by Rick Warren. In his book, Warren shares five ways to live out your purpose. They are as follows: worship, unselfish fellowship, spiritual maturity, your ministry and your mission.

If you and your son are Christian, the first three will resonate with you. When your son knows and worships Christ, it becomes increasingly important to him to find out who he is in Christ. You can help him by sharing pertinent scriptures with him and sharing with him the importance of asking God to direct him through to his purpose. Spiritual maturity is something that comes with time, studying, learning and applying the word to his life. As your son matures, he will find that in order to walk in his purpose, he will not always be able to do popular pastimes like getting high and having relationships with multiple girls. Instead, he will spend his time focused on honing his craft, listening to how he is being directed and following through with his ministry and his mission.

A lot of times we focus on our sons getting a good job or a career. However, when your son understands that his job or career is a segue into his mission, he will better understand the importance of being receptive to what he was created to do. What he was created to do should be the deciding factor that leads him to a job or career choice.

Some young men see celebrities and popular people and try to be like them. But they don't have to be their role models. Continue to observe your son as he matures. See how his eyes light up when he is immersed in something that comes naturally to him. That is how you will find his mission. Help him to find role models who have excelled in the same field of endeavor. Celebrate him for who he is, quirks and all. Help him to appreciate and respect how God made him so he can use his very uniqueness to grow into what he has been called to become.

I realized my purpose at the age of 25, but it took me several years to walk in it. Once your son finds his purpose, help him to not only embrace it, but to nurture and perfect it. Even though I am an international speaker, I still have to study and work to perfect my ministry/mission in order to be the best I can at who I have been called to be. That means practice, perseverance, research, accountability and vulnerability.

Affirm your son daily. Call him what he is to be. Encourage him to affirm himself. If he has no idea who he is, it's going to be tough for him to find out why he exists and what his purpose is. This could lead to him being involved in drugs, gangs, inappropriate conduct, not valuing his life. It is important that you protect your son's thought process by getting him involved in positive activities often and early.

I didn't know what I wanted to do, but I knew I needed to get tougher. I was a target for bullies in my neighborhood. My mom tried something different and got me a membership to the Boys Club. The transition was tough at first because I grew up with all girls and suddenly was around all boys. My mother made suggestions about activities she wanted me in at the club, but I ultimately had to make my own decisions. It eventually became rewarding. There I learned football, basketball, swimming and how to shoot pool.

Eventually, I chose to play football and pursue a professional career in athletics. I worked day and night. I made it all the way to the NFL and got cut by the Minnesota Vikings, so I had to go to plan B. Being a member of The Boys Club all those years had inspired me and I wanted to give back like my mentors, Ralph Dowe, Cliff Green and others who gave so much of themselves to me. It is the influence from the Boys Club that lead me to education. Even though I went through a few careers before I found my way to my purpose, I was being built up to do the work that I am doing now. I'm fulfilled by the work I do speaking to educators and administrators, parents and students. Being a part of the Boys Club played a significant role in me finding my purpose. My mother's persistence in getting me involved led me there.

As you help to guide your son to his purpose, be sure that he knows that finding himself is not difficult, but it requires honesty. He will fail at some things and if he doesn't give up, those failures, believe it or not, will lead him to his successes. Failure is part of learning. We learn more when we fail if we look at the lessons. Don't be so hard on him when he fails and don't allow him to be hard on himself. Encourage him to learn the lessons and pick up where he left off and be willing to move forward, even if it means moving in a different direction.

Training for sports on the college and pro level is much different from grade school and high school and many young men simply can't handle the mental and physical stress on their body and mind that is required. I was one of the few players on my collegiate team that made it into an NFL training camp. After being cut, I realized that remaining in the NFL as long as I'd hope was not my final purpose. It was a hard pill to swallow, but I forged ahead, and changed my plan. Seeking your purpose is an ongoing process. As your son lives, change will occur: his thoughts, his goals and his dreams. I had to move on from that dream to the next one. I thought about going into coaching, but I wanted to walk away from sports altogether to heal from the emotional hurt of being cut as well as the physical wear-and-tear that playing football had done to my body. The road to finding your purpose is funny that way. I often wonder if I hadn't been emotionally and physically hurt and remained in sports, would I have still made my way to my purpose. Either way, I am walking in my purpose now and I know that I am where I am supposed to be.

Use Your Own Experiences

It is vital to talk about your own experiences and dreams with your son. Not enough mothers speak to their sons about their failures, so children grow up thinking that their parents didn't make bad decisions. Today children live in a microwave society in which they want everything right now and are used to getting a lot of things with little effort. Your son must learn to slow down so he understands the process it takes to succeed, while learning to respect it, and appreciate it. Not only should you share your relationship experiences, but even more powerful, you should share your lived experiences with him. Your experiences are a good way of teaching.

Share your story with your son and speak openly and transparently about your failures. Talk to him about how you overcame your failures in work, career, and school. Tell him about your successes and how you accomplished them. Tell him what inspired you, be it a movie, a show, a book, a conversation, or a pivotal moment. Share with him how you failed at or succeeded at putting your dream into motion. Let him know that you are still dreaming. Tell him to do the same, then talk to him about the importance of taking the right steps to realize his dream. If you have them, be transparent with your son about your business and career ventures. Share the highs, lows, and everything in between.

Maybe you started out dreaming about something, and that dream may have changed quickly. In fact, that dream probably changed several times. Hurdle after hurdle may have arisen, whether it was money, loss of interest, time, pregnancy or broken promises. Be honest with your son about your difficulties. Maybe you made bad decisions and had bad study habits while in school. If that hindered you from achieving your goals, let your son know. If he has bad study habits, your truth may be motivation for him to work harder in school. If you started out chasing a goal and it didn't work out, talk to him about why it wasn't successful and what you wish you would have done differently. Let him know if you didn't graduate from high school and how that made you feel. If you graduated, but didn't go to college and wanted to, let him know about your obstacles. Share with him how you adapted and built your life. If you stopped dreaming, tell him that you wished you hadn't. Make a pact to start dreaming and working toward each of your dreams together.

Share with your son which classes were the toughest in school. Let him know how you decided on a career choice, or if you had no plan, but wished you did. If you wanted to quit tell him and share with him why you wanted to quit. Explain what kept you going. If you took your academics seriously, this meant that you made some sacrifices. What were they? Maybe you studied instead of hanging out some weekends. Maybe you lost friends along the way. If you went to college, tell your son if you were relieved to leave your parents' house. If things got tougher for you while you were away at school, let him know. If you went to graduate school, law school, or medical school, how was the transition from college? Your son needs to understand the realistic side of pursuing goals because he will surely experience obstacles along the way.

Talking can only take you so far. Action carries you. Faith without works is dead, and the only place success comes before work is in the dictionary. Don't sugarcoat the work it takes to be successful. Nothing comes easy. Even things that are given to you must be maintained.

Your son needs to grasp that pain and adversity are the biggest motivators for champions. Michael Jordan wouldn't have ever become one of the greatest basketball players of all time if he hadn't been cut from his high school basketball team. This one act motivated him to work harder than ever so that being cut would never be an option again. Feeling pain and hurt can be a tool to greater achievements, and even your son needs to feel both failure and success so that he can ultimately become the best version of himself.

Eliminate and Manage Stress

According to the article "Mothers--and Fathers--Report Mental Physical Health Declines" in *American Psychological Association*, forty-eight percent of the parents said the level of stress in their life has increased compared with before the pandemic. Stress is a state of mental or emotional strain resulting from adverse or very demanding circumstances. Many parents suffer from unaddressed daily stress. It's more challenging to take care of others when you haven't taken care of yourself. Not to mention that your son is on the receiving end of your restless or toxic emotions when you haven't rested your body or mind.

Being aware of and managing your stress level is vital. Maternal stress starts from the time a baby is conceived. Carrying your son to term causes stress to your body. You have a person growing inside of you. Some women don't feel beautiful during pregnancy. After giving birth, others stress about their appearance. Once the child arrives, a mother's entire life is altered. Unfortunately, post-partum depression is high among mothers after the baby is born. Mothers often put the needs of the child ahead of her own. She is on round-the-clock watch with her son, especially when he is a newborn. With long sleepless nights and hormonal changes, some mothers may even forget what day it is. Their sleeping patterns are often totally thrown off. In addition, especially if they are nursing, mothers eat more and some are too exhausted or preoccupied with their new child to fit in working out. In these cases, self-care is ignored.

Fathers chip in to assist but no one does more than Mom or Grandma, from preparing milk to changing diapers to bathing to caring for the well-being of the child. Men don't always understand the stress that mothers experience because they are often busy working or watching from the sidelines. Mother's brains are always working because mothers always feel like there is something that needs to be done and there usually is.

Once their son has grown up and doesn't require as much attention, or needs recognition in a different way, it is still tough for some mothers to make the shift back to taking care of themselves. Often another sibling is born, they have demanding jobs and have the responsibility of managing a household of children and maybe a significant other with an equally busy schedule. Despite the demands, when mothers manage to take better care of themselves, caring for their son is easier. I know that's tough to do when you are in mommy-mode and don't get weekends or holidays off. I get it. Being a mom is a tough job. Nonetheless, being unhealthy can make your life strenuous. Practicing self-care gives you a chance to get things right for yourself and prepares you to better handle the people and issues you will encounter. Your son needs you operating at full, not half or one quarter, capacity.

Caring for Yourself

Caring for yourself is important for both your mental and physical health. With the demands of a career and motherhood every day, it's easy to forget the importance of taking care of yourself properly. Even though you're a mom, always consider your health and well-being. It is vital to do things that pour back into you, allowing you to become refreshed and renewed. The following are strategies to eliminate or limit stress:

How to Eliminate or Limit Stress

1. **Stop trying to remember everything.** Nobody remembers everything. Most people over the age of 40 are forgetful. How do you deal with being forgetful? Write things down. Don't use sticky notes because you will lose them. Write all your notes down in one tablet so that you don't have to look for multiple sticky notes. A paper or electronic tablet or an iPad are all helpful solutions.

2. **Stop trying to please everybody.** Instead of trying to please everybody, please yourself. Sometimes attending to your immediate family is enough work within itself. Often, we try to please people who are ungrateful and unworthy of our time, especially extended family members, some of whom never express gratitude in any way. In some instances, the only time you hear from some of them is when they need something from you. When you need something, they are nowhere to be found. Use your free time to be attentive to your own needs and take time for yourself. Other peoples' emergencies are not your emergencies. Practice random acts of kindness. Help those who are grateful and who you get joy from helping. Pull back from always being available.

3. **Take care of your mind and your body.** Take care of your mind and body by practicing these five things daily: exercise, eat right, meditate, pray, and get rest. Do some form of exercise daily by walking, running, biking, etc. Eating right will require you to let go of some of your favorite foods, especially those that are not good for you. If you know it's not good for you, stop eating it altogether or limit your consumption. Meditate on the word of God, positive affirmations and your positive future. Spend time in prayer daily. Keep yourself centered as often as possible. Rest. Go sit down somewhere and stop wearing yourself out. Get off your feet, turn off your computer and TV. Spend some time outside and watch a sunset or read, relax, or go to sleep.

4. **Don't start your day with false energy.** False energy includes caffeine, donuts, sugar, energy drinks, etc. Beginning your day with coffee is starting your day with false energy. Instead, start your day with fruits, vegetables, and plenty of water. Mentally affirm yourself with positive words and tell yourself, "I got this." Affirmations will give you a much-needed boost of positive energy and uplifting words to feed your spirit. Speak positive words over your life, family, and career every day. Don't manifest negative energy by invoking negative words or thoughts into your mouth and mind.

5. **Talk *to* your problems instead of talking *about* your problems.** There is power in the words that come out of your mouth. You will run into obstacles in your life. Speak out against accepting defeat against those obstacles. Instead of complaining about your problems and obstacles, speak directly to the problem. If you don't have enough money, don't rehearse in your mind, "I don't have enough money to pay my bills." Say instead, "I have an abundance and there is always plenty of money to take care of my family." Work hard to reverse the negative. Instead of constantly saying to yourself, "I am a failure. This is hard." Say instead, "I am a success. Anything worth having is worth working for." Pull away from people in your life that bring you no value and don't encourage you with positive reinforcement. Know that you have inside you the ability to overcome any obstacle that you face. You must first believe it. For every problem, there is a solution. Look for the solutions.

Self-Care Doesn't have to be Expensive

Is your peace being compromised? If something costs you your peace, then it costs too much. Stress and strife are expensive because they can take away your peace and could cost you your life. If someone offered me a million dollars for my peace, I would tell them to keep their money. Nothing on this planet is worth my peace. Nothing should be worth yours either. Finding peace, on the other hand, is very inexpensive. Your peace, once found, is priceless, so protect it at all costs.

Some mothers deal with stress and strife for so long that it seems foreign when there are moments of peace. If this is where you are, you have allowed constant worry to reign too long and it is time for you to allow relief to enter your life by making deliberate changes to make room for peace. Sometimes it's as simple as walking for 30 minutes with your earbuds in, listening to inspirational music or messages, taking a break from the nightly news, finding a quiet place to just stop and think about how you would like your future to look. Take an hour or so to yourself to read a book, the Bible, or watch your favorite show to wind down. Sometimes peace is going to the beach, riding your bike, working out or finding other outings that bring you joy.

Self-care should be consistent, planned and budgeted into your weekly schedule. However, it doesn't have to cost you a thing. You don't have to pay to walk in the park or around your neighborhood by yourself, with your significant other, or even with your children. Exercising in your home or riding your bike is free. On the other hand, going to doctors' visits and taking medication to tackle health issues like heart disease, diabetes, hypertension and headaches can become expensive. Some issues can be addressed or even prevented from happening by taking better care of yourself. When your mind and body are fresh and at peace, you will be in a better mood. You will make better decisions for yourself and for your son.

Find a Balance

If you are a working mother, your job may monopolize a great deal of your time, or you may devote all your time to your young son. If either or both are the case, it can take its toll on you. Washing clothes, getting your son ready for school and bed, giving baths, reading bedtime stories, helping with homework, preparing dinner, driving your son from one activity to the next, and tending to your spouse are all jobs within themselves. The key is finding a balance to make it all work.

To eliminate stress, take one hour to yourself every day. If that is impossible, start with a solid 15 minutes. If your schedule is overwhelming, commit to once every week. As you experience the benefits of that time, work to find more days where there are more accommodating pockets of time. When the kids go to sleep at night, before everyone wakes up in the morning, during your lunch break or while your son is at practice are all opportunities for you to focus on yourself.

Working all day at your job, including working through lunch and coming home to your family at night to work more, sometimes falling asleep fully clothed, is not healthy. Unchecked, your body and/or mind could shut down on you, forcing you to decide whether to remain unhealthy or fight to get your health back. You can prevent pre-mature bad health by balancing your life with a schedule that works for you. Carving out this time should not be an option; it's necessary. Forty-five minutes to three hours in one week to save your sanity isn't asking much. Once you give it a try, you will find that it will be one of the best decisions you have ever made for your life.

A mother, as the nurturer, comforter and backbone, sacrifices more than anyone in the family. Kids tend to lean on Mom more than anyone. That's why taking care of your health should be a priority. Your son needs you around for the big moments in his life and you should want to be around to experience them with him. Excessive stress is the enemy and the enemy loses power when you gain the ability to find peace.

Maintaining Your Appearance

It is important for mothers to figure out ways to maintain their appearance. Unfortunately, so many put time into making sure everyone else in the family looks presentable but then go days without grooming themselves. Slacking on bathing, doing your hair or even getting your nails done due to being exhausted or lack of available time is understandable. However, appearance is often tied to self-esteem. You don't have to look like a celebrity every time you walk out of your house, but you could benefit from finding a system that works to keep you presentable enough to feel good about yourself.

Self-love is loving yourself through your flaws. What is on the inside counts, but it is also necessary to look in the mirror to get dressed every day. When doing so, a lot of women judge themselves by their outward appearance. That is why loving who you see looking back at you no matter how many kids you have; no matter how much your body and face have changed is vital. You must see both your inner and outer beauty. If you don't feel good about yourself, it shows. It effects your mood, your self-esteem and your interaction with others. It's time to get your sexy on; your professionalism on; your natural beauty on! Whatever works for you and makes you feel good about yourself, it is time to reconnect to it. Put on your makeup, weave and eye lashes. Wash and go, flat iron, curl your hair or cut it all off. Just get back to you.

Maintaining a positive appearance helps you to prepare to face your day. It prepares you to interact with people in confidence. You never know who you may run into when you leave the house. You may stop by a coffee shop and run into a business contact you've hoped to connect with. If you are single, you may go to your son's school for a meeting and encounter a single father waiting on his daughter. You may meet a lifelong friend at a party. If you stay ready by maintaining your appearance and mental stability, you will not only look prepared, but you'll feel prepared.

Maintaining a positive appearance while married is just as important as when you met your husband. Marriage isn't an excuse to discontinue maintaining your appearance. Don't become complacent. As the old saying goes, "Do the same things that got him in the first place." Don't give up on the habits that attracted your significant other to you. More importantly, look beautiful for yourself.

Find an Accountability Partner

It is tough for a team of one to succeed and retain sustainability. You can't do it all alone, even if you are a "supermom." It is helpful to partner with another mother who is also attempting to incorporate self-care into her life or a mother who has already gone through this season. A good partner understands and respects your goals and will be a good sounding board. A good accountability partner will help you to remain committed, focused and consistent. The person should be someone you can vent to and who can relate to your daily struggles.

The two of you will hold each other accountable in matters of work, family, health, wellness or personal goals. If you want to lose weight and get fit by taking aerobics on Tuesdays and Thursdays, your accountability partner will call to encourage you to go to class on time or may even show up to do it with you. You should do the same for her. Making it a priority to find and make a pact with an accountability partner, will give you the extra boost that you need on your journey to improving your self-care.

BIBLIOGRAPHY

FOR MOTHERS RAISING SONS

Bibliography

Beqiri, Gini. "The 5 Features of Emotional Intelligence." *VirtualSpeech.com*, September 9, 2018. https://virtualspeech.com/blog/5-features-emotional-intelligence.

Cikanavicius, Darius. "The Effects of Trauma from Growing Up Too Fast." *PsychCentral*, December 8, 2019. https://psychcentral.com/blog/psychology_self/2019/12/trauma-growing-up-fast#5.

Cinelli, Elisa. "8-Year-Old Child Development Milestones: Your child's growth and development at age 8." *Verywell Family*, March 15, 2022. https://www.verywellfamily.com/8-year-old-developmental-milestones-620729.

Cooper, Alexia and Erica L. Smith. "Homicide Trends in the United States, 1980-2008: Annual Rates for 2009 and 2010." *Bureau of Justice Statistics*, U.S. Department of Justice, November 2011, https://bjs.ojp.gov/content/pub/pdf/htus8008.pdf.

Creflo Dollar Ministries. "Understanding Grace Based Relationships – Sunday Service." *YouTube Video*, 1:17:36, https://www.youtube.com/watch?v=WkGKPosi3N0.

Emory University Health Sciences Center, March 16, 2004, https://www.sciencedaily.com/releases/2004/03/040316072953.htm.

Fahey, Jacqueline E. "The Impact of the Mother-Son Relationship on Expressions of Aggression in Young Adulthood." Ph.D. Diss., Alliant International University, 2018. *ProQuest Dissertations*, https://www.proquest.com/openview/d0a833d306790f35dee1d42223824f8e/1.pdf?pqorigsite=gscholar&cbl=18750.

"Fathers' Roles in the Care and Development of Their Children: The Role of Pediatricians," *Pediatrics* (2016) 138 (1): e20161128. https://doi.org/10.1542/peds.2016-1128.

"Half of All Teens Feel Uncomfortable Talking to Their Parents About Sex While Only 19 Percent of Parents Feel the Same, New Survey Shows." *Planned Parenthood Federation of America,* October 2, 2012. Last updated March 11, 2016,
https://www.plannedparenthood.org/about-us/newsroom/press-releases/half-all-teens-feel-uncomfortable-talking-their-parents-about-sex-while-only-19-percent-parents#:~:text=Half%20(50%20percent)%20of%20all,it%20comes%20to%20discussing%20sex.

"Heart Disease and African Americans." *U.S. Department of Health and Human Services Office of Minority Health.* Last updated January 31, 2022.
https://minorityhealth.hhs.gov/omh/browse.aspx?lvl=4&lvlid=19.

Hill, Amelia. "Most Mums Admit Favouring Sons, Say Researchers." *The Guardian,* October 5, 2010.
https://www.theguardian.com/society/2010/oct/06/most-mums-favour-sons-survey.

Houston, Elaine, B.Sc. "The Importance of Emotional Intelligence (Incl. Quotes)." *Positive Psychology.com,* February 6, 2019. https://positivepsychology.com/importance-of-emotional-intelligence/

"Kids and Teens: Developmental Milestones." *John Hopkins Medicine.* https://www.hopkinsmedicine.org/health/wellness-and-prevention/kids-and-teens-developmental-milestones.

Krahé, B., Scheinberger-Olwig, R., & Bieneck, S. "Men's reports of nonconsensual sexual interactions with women: Prevalence and impact." *Archives of Sexual Behavior 32* (2003): 165–175. https://doi.org/10.1023/A:1022456626538.

"Limerence," n. *Lexico*, (2022). Accessed March 15, 2022, https://www.lexico.com/en/definition/limerence.

"Mothers – and fathers – report mental, physical health declines." *American Psychological Association*. March 11, 2011. www.apa.org/news/press/releases/stress/2021/one-year-pandemic-stress-parents.

New International Version. *Biblica*, 2011. Bible.com. Web. 2011

Obuchi, Chie, Sayaka Ogane, Yuki Sato, and Kimitaka Kaga, "Auditory symptoms and psychological characteristics in adults with auditory processing disorders," *National Library of Medicine*, May 15, 2017, https://www.ncbi.nlm.nih.gov/pmc/articles/PMC5963468/.

Pratt, Kim LCSW, "Psychology Tools: What is Anger? A Secondary Emotion." *Healthy Psych*. February 3, 2014, https://healthypsych.com/psychology-tools-what-is-anger-a-secondary-emotion/

Robbins, Harvey. *How to Speak and Listen Effectively*. American Management Association, 1992.

Savage, Mark. "R. Kelly: The History of Allegations Against Him." *BBC News*, September 28, 2021,
https://www.bbc.com/news/entertainment-arts-40635526.

"Stress," n., 1a. *The Britannica Dictionary*, (2022). Accessed March 15, 2022, https://www.britannica.com/dictionary/stress#:~:text=a%20%5Bnoncount%5D%20%3%20a%20state,in%20response%20to%20emotional%20stress.

"Tweens." *Verywell Family*, March 24, 2022. https://www.verywellfamily.com/tweens-4157364.

"Understanding Child Trauma." *SAMHSA*, Last updated January 11, 2022. https://www.samhsa.gov/child-trauma/understanding-child-trauma.

Warren, Rick. *The Purpose Driven Life*. Zondervan, 2002.

"Your Son at 18 and Beyond: Milestones." *Grow by WebMD*, March 6, 2021. https://www.webmd.com/parenting/guide/son-18-beyond-milestones.

Books by
Robert Jackson

No More Excuses:

The Curriculum

Becoming The Educator They Need

ASCD, 2019
Stock #119010
ISBN 978-1-4166-2820-0
Retail: $24.95

The Workbook for Girls

Lavelle Publishing, 2016
Pub Date: November, 2016
Paperback, 86 pages
ISBN: 978-0-9659254-6-4
Retail: $13.99

Educating Black & Latino Males

Lavelle Publishing, 2012
Pub Date: July, 2012
Paperback, 192 pages
ISBN: 978-0-9659254-5-7
Retail: $23.99

Put a Stop to Bullying

Lavelle Publishing, 2012
Pub Date: June, 2012
Paperback, 72 pages
ISBN: 978-0-9659254-6-4
Retail: $14.99

Black Men Stand Up!

Lavelle Publishing, 2008
Pub Date: May 23, 2008
Paperback, 180 pages
ISBN: 978-0-9659254-1-9
Retail: $15.00

The Workbook for Boys

Lavelle Publishing, 2009
Second Edition: April 2022
Paperback, 72 pages
ISBN: 978-0-9659254-8-8
Retail: $15.00

Special Discounts when Purchased in Bulk
For Premiums and Sales Promotions
as well as for Fundraising or Educational Purposes
contact info@robertjacksonmotivates.com

Order your copies today!

www.robertjacksonmotivates.com

About Robert Jackson

"For every problem, there is a solution" is Robert's motto. Jackson began his teaching career 27 years ago in Indianapolis Public Schools after being cut from the NFL Minnesota Vikings in 1995. He has become one of the most sought-after speakers in the country, delivering keynote addresses and workshops to educators, administrators, parents and students. Mr. Jackson has written and published 7 books and has written articles for ASCD's Educational Leadership Magazine. His ASCD book, *Becoming the Educator They Need: Strategies, Mindsets, and Beliefs for Supporting Male Black and Latino Students* won the Gold Excel Award for Technical Writing.

He attended Western Kentucky University where he received his BS Degree in Industrial Technology while lettering 4 years in both Football and Track. He has keynoted and conducted workshops at national conferences including ASCD, ESEA, CAAASA, NABSE, SREB, Innovative Schools Summit, AMLE and AASA. Mr. Jackson has received numerous awards for his work. He is a Life Member of Kappa Alpha Psi Fraternity Inc. and the NFL Players Association.

LinkedIn
https://www.linkedin.com/in/robert-jackson-85120735/

Facebook
https://www.facebook.com/Robjnupe

Facebook Fan Page
https://www.facebook.com/groups/robertjacksonmotivates/about/

Twitter
@RJmotivates

Instagram
@robjmotivates

Website
www.robertjacksonmotivates.com

Email
robert@robertjacksonmotivates.com

Robert Jackson

Consultant/Speaker

Robert Jackson can tailor his presentations to meet the needs of your staff, students and parents. His workshops, keynotes and presentations are very interactive. Mr. Jackson offers service packages for school districts that include stand-alone presentations, and/or a series of professional development trainings to continually engage your staff, students and parents throughout the year. This training includes assemblies, workshops and keynotes. The sessions, along with his curriculum, will energize your students, staff, and parents to work together to bridge the gap and produce more successful students.

Workshops & Presentations

Educators/Administrators

Building Cultural Awareness with Staff/Students
Strategies to Educating Black and Latino Males
Conflict Resolution/Team Building
Building Healthy Relationships with Students and Staff
Effective Leadership for Administrators
Self-care and Mental Health Awareness for Staff
Social/Emotional Learning
Restorative Practices
Bullying Prevention
Working with Students with Behavioral Issues
Working with Students and Staff Who have Experienced Trauma

Parents

Solutions & Strategies for Mothers Raising Sons
Helping Your Child Become More Disciplined and Responsible
Do's and Don'ts for Parenting Young Men/Women
Bullying Awareness for Parents (Child Being Bullied/is a Bully)
Overcoming Anger, Abuse, and Anxiety
Healthy Relationships
Fatherhood Training (For Men)

Students

Top 10 Rules of a Successful Student
Discipline and Accountability
Steps to Being a Successful Student In and Out of The Classroom
Education vs. Athletics
Bullying Prevention
Anger Management (How do I overcome it?)
Dressing for Success/Hygiene Awareness
Self-Esteem & Loving Yourself
Coping with Peer Pressure
Manhood Training for Male Students
How to Overcome Trauma
Mental Health, Let's Talk

Mr. Robert Jackson empowered my entire faculty and staff through professional development, and most importantly, my elementary scholars. His presentations allowed for awareness that we have a problem, that we can make a difference, and unequivocally emphasized, 'No More Excuses', as he shared the solution(s). His message was thought provoking, mind changing, and left us with real strategies, equipping us with the necessary tools to make an impact on our youth!"

–Dr. Roslyn Vaughn, Principal
Anderson Elementary Dual
Language School
Houston, Texas

To Book Robert Jackson
Visit: www.robertjacksonmotivates.com

Mr. Jackson, thanks for being our Keynote speaker. You are the ultimate professional and you are very passionate about your work. Your presentation style is engaging and motivating - you have a unique ability to connect with your audience. After listening to you, my staff was ready to start the school year with the right mindset. Thanks for helping us to "set the tone" for what has been a very good school year.

– Dr. Marc Smith, Superintendent
Duncanville ISD

Robert's Motto is:

FOR EVERY PROBLEM
THERE IS A SOLUTION

www.robertjacksonmotivates.com